T0198921

BATTLING FROM
GLORY
TO
GLORY

ANDREA FURULI

WESTBOW
PRESS®
A DIVISION OF THOMAS NELSON
& ZONDERVAN

This book is a work of non-fiction. Unless otherwise noted, the author
and the publisher make no explicit guarantees as to the accuracy of
the information contained in this book and in some cases, names of
people and places have been altered to protect their privacy.

WestBow Press books may be ordered through booksellers or by contacting:

WestBow Press
A Division of Thomas Nelson & Zondervan
1663 Liberty Drive
Bloomington, IN 47403
www.westbowpress.com
1 (866) 928-1240

Because of the dynamic nature of the Internet, any web addresses or
links contained in this book may have changed since publication and
may no longer be valid. The views expressed in this work are solely those
of the author and do not necessarily reflect the views of the publisher,
and the publisher hereby disclaims any responsibility for them.

Any people depicted in stock imagery provided by Getty Images are
models, and such images are being used for illustrative purposes only.
Certain stock imagery © Getty Images.

ISBN: 978-1-9736-8379-7 (sc)
ISBN: 978-1-9736-8380-3 (hc)
ISBN: 978-1-9736-8378-0 (e)

Library of Congress Control Number: 2020900623

Print information available on the last page.

WestBow Press rev. date: 02/14/2020

Contents

Dedication ix
Preface xi

Season of True North

PART ONE

Wedding Anniversary.. 1
Home Adjustment.. 3
What Next?... 4

Season of Chaos

Sideways... 7
Oahu Bound 10
Have Faith 12
Power Granny 14
Surprise!... 16
A Miracle 18
Meet Furuli Baby Number Three... 20
Faith Filling 22
Routine Day Trips... 24
Get Lost!... 26
Dejavu 28
Wake Up Call 31
Home Away From Home 33
Weekend Cruiser... 35
House Dads Are Cool 37

Storing Our Treasures 39
Got Activities? 41
Return To Work 43
Science VS. Screws 44
Youtube + Home Depot = Boy Genius 46
Squealing 49
Bike Booboo 50
They Know 62
Just Hang On 65
Who Needs Disney? 67
Framily 69
Hormones 70

Season of Uncertainty

No, Not Again! 75
Do You Remember? 79
No Matter What 81
Bracing Again 82
Family Meeting 84
Departure 86
Time To Get Up 88
Flashback: Down She Went 90
Laughter Is Good Medicine 92
Got Me An Angel 93
He Is Well 95
Bat Cave 97
Meals And Medications 99
Naps 100

Season of True North

PART TWO

Lost And Found 105
Charades 106
Creature Of Habit 109

Stripe Head 111
Word And Number Play 113
Cheers And Tears 115
Success 117

Season Ahead

Go On 121

Acknowledgments 123

Dedication

To Kevin, all the love, appreciation and respect in the world for the toughest and most tender guy I know.

To Phoebe, Ian, and Jonah, my three most treasured gems here on earth.

To my mom, and the special heaven-sent angels whose love covered and sustained me.

May God's sovereign strength and infinite love be shown through the slivers of my story and provide a source of hope, courage, strength, and inspiration.

Preface

As a child, I was afraid of the unseen and the mention of ghosts would keep me up at night. But today, as a wife and mom of three children, I'd challenge any ghost, anywhere in exchange for taking away the ugly reality of brain cancer that has haunted my family for over fifteen years.

My adult nightmares include things like MRI results, health insurance authorizations, and the silent anxiety of waiting - waiting for test results, a phone call from the doctor, whether my husband's memory will be intact after surgery, or if his speech will improve. These are the thoughts that keep me up at night.

Then suddenly, I didn't want to wait or sink deeper into the personal vulnerability mud pit. I realized that my lens of a wife and a mom were calling me forward to share my story of being a caregiver, advocate, protector, provider, and nurturer to and for my family. I felt moved hugely and believed that I'm destined to come out of my corner to deliver a tender-tough message of hope and perseverance that has blessed my family profoundly. It is a personal story of battling from glory to glory.

Our story is not over nor is life ever stable for very long. I am still on this very real and raw journey, but cannot wait any longer to begin sharing the struggles and the triumphs. My prayer is that it might help someone who needs to believe in hope and know without a doubt that God is real, God is love, and God is in control.

To begin to understand our journey and the accompanying wounds and scars requires a deeper look at where we came from.

Season of True North

PART ONE

Wedding Anniversary

The air felt heavy with moisture and a hint of rain as we deplaned. The thought of a mist with little droplets soothed my nerves; it was a long flight, and I was cramped and edgy the entire way. I looked forward to the promise of a damp blanketing of Hilo rain and knew it would cleanse us. I meant me - cleanse me of the weighted anxiety as I accompanied my husband home from San Francisco.

Fellow passengers may have observed that I was approaching fifty, in decent physical shape, of modest means and happily married. I was make-up free except for lip balm. There were also signs of wrinkles feeling right at home at the outside corners of my eyes and soft grays at my temples. I wore stretchy pants layered with a couple of long-sleeved sweaters, and my feet were enjoying a brand new pair of walking shoes. On my lap sat a worn hand-me-down red backpack that contained a gallon-sized Zip Loc bag filled with medications. I held Kevin's left hand as he rested it atop of the backpack; on my other hand, I wore my wedding ring. Today was our eighteenth anniversary.

Kevin and I took our time and walked slowly down to the baggage claim area and made our way curbside with suitcases in tow. I looked over at him and felt so relieved that we made it home. I knew how exhausted he must have felt, but there he was, insistent that a wheelchair was unnecessary. He walked slowly and the mild dragging of his weaker right leg was hardly noticeable. In fact, without the white cloth peeking out from beneath his hat, there was no obvious way of knowing that my husband had his fourth brain surgery less than a week ago.

It was late afternoon and it had been two weeks since we left for San Francisco. It seemed surreal to be back home. We were excited to be reunited with our family and I powered my phone and confirmed that the kids were nearby and coming around the bend at the airport. Then I saw our van approaching like a big blue-gray whale finding its way to us in slow motion. I was on hyper-happy mode, and stood there like a giddy kid, waiting for a celebrity arrival. Finally, the van parked in front of our noses and one by one the kids opened the doors and hopped out to greet us.

Phoebe made her way from the driver's seat and was quick to say, "Dad, you look good!" I could feel my eyes start to get hot and teary and tried to blink back the waterworks. I was so happy to see them. There were hugs and more hugs, a quick family picture and then we loaded up. Phoebe drove home, while Kevin rode shotgun and I sat in the back with Ian and Jonah. I enjoyed the chatter and gritted my teeth as Kevin whipped off his hat to show the boys his stitches, affectionately nicknamed "T-Bone" by Ian. The Frankenstein-like sutures make me queasy, but, my husband is a champ, and the kids deserve to know and appreciate this. So, I kept my mouth shut, rolled my eyes, leaned back to take in my family posse, and what it means to be part of it.

I nestled in my seat and felt myself breathe in and out, purposely, trying to calm myself with all of the big emotions swirling around in my head. The layers of worry began to peel away as I relaxed in my familiar space. It felt nice to be in the mom Van. And then, a super loud growl erupted from my tummy, demanding to be heard, after being ignored all day. Inside my head, I thanked God for watching over the kids and equipping them to be brave and courageous. Then I said, *"So what's for dinner?"*

Home Adjustment

It was a huge relief to be back with family and friends, surrounded by things that comforted me. Even the wobbly railing I held to walk upstairs and the incessant yappy dog in the yard reminded me that I was on my turf and now had a home team advantage.

I had not yet fully processed our most recent trip to UC San Francisco Medical Center. It was an awkward time and space for me; after all, *this was the second time we were there for brain surgery in six months*. Kevin initially went through an "awake surgery" in August 2018 where a surgical team talked to him during the operation to monitor progress. The surgery was successful, yet cancer returned two months later. We headed back to battle this demon and take it out again in February 2019. Kevin made it through and here we were blessed to figure out life after brain surgery number four.

I was grateful beyond measure, but, my reserves were depleted and I was just tired of it all. I felt so deeply appreciative and optimistic one moment, then weary and flat out depressed the next. The most recent span of events was especially harrowing, with just a brief moment of pause to rest and catch my breath. The peaks and valleys of life happen, but I've usually found time to rest in between. But this time, the intensity of life seemed brutal; one battle after another and it was taking a toll on Kevin, on me, and my whole family.

What Next?

When I think ahead, I feel apprehensive and force my way back to the present – right here, right now.

I am blessed to be here and have a sense of peace, sort of. I want to hold on to this sense, knowing that it is temporary, for as long as I can. I want to savor this state-of-mind because I can remember, like it was yesterday, when it was quite the contrary; when my life felt anything **but** calm and peaceful.

Season of Chaos

Sideways

Our family history began fifteen years earlier.

It was early January 2005. I was thirty-four at the time and Kevin was forty. We had a young family; Phoebe was a big sister at age three to Ian, a six-month-old teething ball of wet-stinky drool. Kevin had started his own mobile diesel mechanics repair business, and settled into his work groove, servicing customers across the island. I also began a new job as an office manager for The Nature Conservancy and enjoyed an hour-long solo commute to Waimea. Many folks found this daily drive time to be crazy, but it was *my time* to enjoy the radio or pure peace.

During the workweek, I dashed out in the morning to drop off baby Ian with my mom and left Kevin to get Phoebe ready and take her to preschool before clocking billable work hours. We were both hardworking and driven, running full speed in our professional pursuits and trying to figure out parenting roles. We were busy and our days were full.

Fortunately for my family, we also had a special secret weapon - my mom. Granny, as my kids call her, has always been an integral part of our family and given unconditionally of herself in more ways than I can ever fully describe. She'd receive a little infant early in the morning and share highlights of their day when I picked Ian up later in the afternoon. She was the bedrock that I've relied on for safekeeping, comfort, solace, advice, and love, always.

Life seemed normal and predictable before it went completely sideways. Kevin and I had met, fell in love, had our first and second kid, and started on this family adventure. As new and slightly older first-time parents, we were figuring out what it meant to work and raise a family. Our adult priorities shifted drastically from making sure beer was in the refrigerator for after work, to buying a case of diapers and bottle formula on the way home. Then one day, everything came to a crazy, screeching halt and my life changed again, forever.

While at work, I answered a call from my husband's friend Greg. My boss Rob heard a one-sided conversation that went a little like this: *"What?! What do you mean he was on the ground? Is he okay? Where is he now? Tell him to go to the Emergency Room, now, or I'll drag him there myself!"*

Rob rushed over to my desk and asked me what was going on. I remembered feeling completely panicked and said I wasn't sure but had to leave! I told him a friend called to say he went to see Kevin who was working on a backhoe parked at our home and found him unconscious on the ground. Kevin awoke angry and agitated. He went upstairs and walked into the house to lay down with his work boots still on.

I convinced my boss that I was able to drive and promised to call him with an update. On my drive back to Hilo, I called on the big guns – my mom. I asked her to go over to my home about fifteen minutes away from her to see what was going on. I tasked her with taking Kevin to the hospital if he refused to go on his own, and I would meet them there. Bad, bad thoughts coursed through my mind as I drove, like, *What could've caused him to fall? Was he drinking? Was he doing drugs? Maybe both? Did he suffer a concussion?* The alone drive time I used to treasure felt ominous and oppressive.

I met my husband in the Emergency Room, and by then, he convinced the doctor that he felt fine and didn't need to wait for the CT machines to be fixed. Machines were broken and had been for a while. He had not taken any type of scan up to that point and accepted the story he created that he must have slipped and fallen from the machine he was working on. It was unsettling. I asked the doc if there was anything else that could've been overlooked. *I thought we're both of Filipino ancestry and our families have a history of diabetes. Can we blame this on sugar?*

I needed an explanation of what happened and wasn't ready to accept that he probably just slipped, fell, was left unconscious, but now fine and back to normal. There was no bump on his head, or bruise on his shoulder, so the story didn't make sense. With his cocky indignant voice, Kevin looked at me and said something, like "c'mon, enough already…let's just go!" He oozed macho-man-sass and made sure we all knew how inconvenienced he was, how overbearing I was acting, and how silly this whole situation was. To think that I almost gave in makes me shake. We were all tired, grumpy and frazzled over what seemed like a whole lot of nothing. Then the CT machine was fixed, Kevin was whisked away and a scan was done. This was divine intervention.

I remembered how the doc averted eye contact when he walked into our room after hours of waiting. My eyes locked on to his tall figure and followed his brisk steps as he put the scans up on the dimly lit holder on the wall. He flipped the light switch off and pointed to the illuminated scan and said matter-of-factly, that Kevin had a brain tumor.

Bam! Just like that. I was shocked and said nothing; mention of surgery was the last thing I remembered.

Oahu Bound

The local Emergency Room Doc had already contacted a neurosurgeon on Oahu and Kevin was set to be flown ASAP to Queen's Medical Center. But the weather was extremely stormy and Hilo was experiencing a deluge of rainfall mixed with thunder and lightning, so the flight departure was delayed for a day. Already a nervous flyer, I had to face this new threat now defined as "brain surgery" that nearly pushed me over the edge. My anxiety levels were so intense that I couldn't tell you my name or birthday. I left Phoebe and Ian, with my parents, so I could focus, but the truth was that I could barely hold myself together. They were safe and Phoebe was content knowing she was having a sleepover. By then I was on "autopilot" and went home to pack a bag of clothes, then headed right back to the hospital, where Kevin was moved out of the ER to another room overnight.

The next day, two men arrived at Kevin's bedside and wheeled him directly to the ambulance that delivered him to the Medivac Airplane at the airport. We were later met by an ambulance on the ground in Honolulu and taken directly to the hospital. There we met his neurosurgeon. I felt at ease with him immediately. He was the guy I was forced to entrust to cut into Kevin's skull and remove a tumor. It was an awful whirlwind that picked me up, stripped me from all things happy and safe and slammed me to the ground where I remained numb, lonely and scared.

Kevin underwent brain surgery number one in January 2005.

His doc referred to the procedure as a "craniotomy" and the sound of it made me cringe. On the day of surgery, I was allowed to spend time with Kevin up until they gave him anesthesia and the surgeon explained that it would be about 4 hours. I don't recall how long it was, but remembered how my heart jumped out of my body when I saw him walking down the hallway in his scrubs looking for me. He looked in my eyes and told me Kevin was ok.

Thank God, the surgery was successful. I barely left his side from the Intensive Care Unit to his transition to the patient floor. The only time I would leave him was late in the evening to walk to the rental unit on hospital grounds to shower and make phone calls. I was so insecure, and certain that something would happen to him in my absence. My solitary walks between his room and the rental units were probably the saddest memories I have stored in my psyche. I felt completely overwhelmed and sadness forced me to weep until I made it to the room where I would break down and sob. Rarely were there others walking late at night, so there in the dark, my sorrow would often bubble up from down deep and overflow. I missed my family and friends intensely.

Have Faith

Life turned completely upside down. Everything happened so quickly with barely any time to process; my husband lay in a hospital bed, our kids were in Hilo with my parents, and I was alone. Heavy-hearted and scared, I was forced to face thoughts that brought me to my knees. I remembered the guilt I felt when I thought our situation was punishment; karma for ugly things that I did in my past, evil thoughts I entertained and past grudges I held on to. I was at life's lowest of lows and it was then when I would repeat silently to myself in my mind, over and over, *please let Kevin be healed, please, please, please let Kevin be healed.* In the ICU, I held his hand and begged for healing as I looked at the crimson-red bandage on his head. In his room with the lights dimmed, again, I begged for healing and lay my head next to his pillow while he slept. My mind would wander to the kids and I begged that Kevin be healed and able to spend more time with them.

One night as I braced for my walk to the rental unit, I began my desperate mantra-like plea and whispered, *please, please, please let Kevin be healed.* I left his room and snaked down the hallways to the sidewalk connecting the hospital with Manamana Apartments. As much as I was afraid of leaving Kevin alone, I was equally afraid of being by myself in the dark. I'd repeat the prayer silently and it would soothe me and offer a safe space and time to cry. Focused on the words in my head, and the sidewalk ahead, I heard words spoken back to me in response to my plea for healing. I heard, *"have faith and your prayers will be answered."*

I was too afraid to stop, but slowed down and looked side to side, and again, side to side trying to make sense of what I heard. It was dark, still and quiet with absolutely no foot traffic. I can't say I felt mighty and empowered, but admit to feeling puzzled. I strained to hear more, but that was it. I was confident that I heard what I heard. This was my holy moment and it rocked my world. Kevin later asked me, "what did you hear, what did 'it' sound like?" I looked into his eyes and thought deeply before I confessed "I'm not sure. I think it was spoken inside of my head." "But what did it sound like?" he asked and was met with my prickly, "I heard what I heard, but I don't know what it sounded like." *Why was that so hard to understand?*

Something happened inside me that night. I felt despair and a loneliness so deep without a loved one in sight. Then I *sensed* warm words that urged me to have "faith" when I had no idea what faith meant. Up until then, I had never identified with a religion, experienced Sunday services, knew Jesus, or read scripture. But during my walk, there was a marvelous connection that took place. I believe Jesus walked alongside me and made his presence known; someone knew my story and cared about me, and my soul was encouraged.

Power Granny

It is difficult to express the joy and gratitude I felt when my mom flew over to visit Kevin after his surgery. My mom, the ultimate power granny, packed up Phoebe and Ian and flew over to visit us at the hospital two days after the procedure. At the time, we had not seen the kids for nearly a week. She bravely assembled the necessary items needed to accompany a toddler and baby, jumped on an airplane, rented a van and stayed overnight at the rental unit that I barely occupied. A feat I wouldn't have done myself unless forced to. But, my mom knew how broken we felt and came with the healing reinforcements we desperately needed.

I perked up when I heard Phoebe's very distinct little lady voice. I stood and peeked out of Kevin's hospital room as they made their way to us. My heart broke when I saw her bouncing down the hall with my mom trailing behind her with Ian in her arms. Phoebe rushed into the room and I gently lifted her to sit next to her dad in the bed, and then tearfully watched her uneasy gaze settle on his swollen face and turban-like bandages wrapped around his head.

It was tense and difficult to watch her try to make sense of what was going on. What started as a visit that would take her to someplace new and exciting, turned into more of a *"where am I and what happened to my dad?"* scene from a scary kid movie. But all that tension melted with Ian as the main and very welcome distraction. He lightened the mood as he took center stage and slobbered, grunted and bounced while being held, non-stop. He was beyond crawling and the threat of being an early walker was imminent. Oh, it felt so good to have them here, even if only for a couple of days.

Surprise!

Healing and recovery went exceptionally well after Kevin's surgery and the neurosurgeon told us that the entire tumor was removed and there was a clear margin. My interpretation went something like - *all the toxic tissue was removed and a little extra brain matter was taken out just to make sure.*

Kevin felt good, in fact, really good. I could tell he was in pain, but he was able to get up and practice walking a couple of days later. He could also communicate well and regained his arrogant edge pretty quickly. He seemed to be more preoccupied with the titanium tools that the surgeon used to cut his skull open with than anything else. He was overly impressed with these tools and was genuinely upset with me because I didn't ask the doctor if we could take the tools home. *Messed up, right?!* You might guess what I wanted to tell him he could do with those titanium tools.

Years later, I can understand how this macho posturing may have been Kevin's way of coping; a distraction from the ugly trauma that was in his face. I have an aversion and think "stupid tools," but perhaps it represented a psychological trophy or something to my husband? Like an animal stuffed by a taxidermist, perhaps the titanium tinker toy could have represented something that was conquered and worthy of hanging on a wall. Again, I'm quite the opposite and wouldn't flinch if I never saw the invasive tools ever. *What for?*

Physicians who made up a "tumor board" met after the surgery to review pathology reports and discuss follow up plans. In Kevin's case, the consensus amongst the physicians was that he would not need treatment, other than follow up MRIs. *Praise God!* This was good news, like really good news, because we just received confirmation that I was pregnant with Furuli Baby number three on the way.

A Miracle

I sensed something was up and went to Dr. Dolan's earlier to take a pregnancy test. In a flash, results were in and I knew for certain that life was about to take us on more twists and turns.

I wish I could say how joy-filled I was. But I can't, because I wasn't joy-filled at all. I was scared, really scared, while news sunk in that I had a little innocent and precious baby growing inside of me. I felt helpless having just stepped through this invasive cut into your husband's skull kind of surgery, and then discovered that I'm pregnant shortly after. This baby didn't have a choice of what family he/she would be born into or future circumstances he/she would face. Looking back, I cannot fathom how I faced knowing that I would soon be a mom of three and spouse to a brain cancer survivor.

I was lost and needed to deal with the junk that occupied my daily thoughts. You know, the ugly kind of thoughts that I'm talking about? The kind that can make your heart beat scary fast and lodge a painful ache in your throat to block sobs from finding release from a broken heart. That's what I remembered feeling like for a good portion of my pregnancy. I felt worried and then later felt guilty for even having such feelings.

I also couldn't shake the subtle threat to Kevin's health that seemed to linger around our daily life. I was afraid of the tumor coming back, then having to face the possibility of raising my kids solo, with number three on the way. This fear was like a nagging source of dread that occupied my psyche, and it had a powerful influence on my attitude; it was horrid. I was a worrywart and always have been. I wore an invisible coat of worry, like mild vog that you can faintly smell, and causes your eyes to tear, and nose to wrinkle. It's not visible, but present enough to be a nuisance. Pregnancy was difficult, and I had to work hard at thinking positive thoughts and to counter-battle worry and discouraging "what if's" to let my baby grow peacefully so that he/she would be born at the right time, happy and healthy.

My body geared up for baby production all over again and I was a T-I-R-E-D. I continued with my daily hour-plus commute to work, while Kevin was forced to rely on others to drive him to and from work. But catch this - he was working! He was able to gradually return to work on repair projects and was blessed to have someone provide a ride throughout his driving restriction period. Law banned him from driving for six months after his surgery. I remembered feeling consumed by my woe is me attitude - *poor me, pregnant and doomed for who knows what awaits me right around the corner.*

I had very little mama bear reserves on hand to lavish on the kids. At home, Phoebe was pretty easy to please and contentedly sat by herself with a book. Ian required energy, and I was in short supply as he started to walk and explore more and more. I'd look at the two of them at the end of the day and should've scooted over to sit with them and open up that big green book of Mother Goose Rhymes to read. I didn't. I was slow-moving, fat and fatigued, and had a difficult time holding Ian on my lap with a bulging belly. It was especially rough trying to keep up with Ian whose high-intensity impish nature had him walking before he was one and always, *in constant motion.* Ian was his daddy's boy. Thankfully, where I lacked in pouring affection, Kevin made up for by carrying, playing and holding Ian and Phoebe close when it mattered.

Meet Furuli Baby Number Three

Our newest addition, Jonah Lee Furuli was born less than a year after Kevin's brain surgery.

Life got a little more interesting with another little "human bean" in the family. We transitioned to a van to accommodate yet another car seat and purchased a dual stroller; the kind for twins. Life seemed to revolve around formula, breastfeeding, and diapers, boxes and boxes of diapers. Daily routines consisted of feeding, cleaning, repeat, times three. It was exhausting and it took every bit of energy I had to take care of the immediate needs of these three unique *littles*, even with my mom as back up.

HGTV and the Cooking Channels were my lifelines with a newborn. I treasured the sacred time when I nursed Jonah in bed while watching countless hours of House Hunters and Rachel Ray's Cooking Show. One day I was in bed during the day napping with Jonah cradled on one side, with the TV on in the background. All was well. Then all of a sudden, I heard the annoying sound of a lawnmower starting up. After several unsuccessful cranks, it growled to life and the neighbor next door proceeded to mow the lawn. I was mad! Seriously, I thought why was someone obnoxious enough to invade my quiet time to mow midday during the week? By now Jonah woke up and started to cry. I rolled over and yanked open the louvers loudly and caught the attention of the mower. She looked up at me through the louvers and said, "Oh, I'm sorry...." I scowled, closed the window, picked up my baby and found my way to the living room where I was forced to settle for the lumpy sofa.

Kevin thankfully had been cleared to drive and was back to work. He never really fully stopped. Mechanic services were in demand, and drivers would pick him up and take him home from work when he was temporarily unable to drive himself. He was fortunate that one company relied on him full time and provided our family with a stable income.

Our life was stable, sort of, because of the chaos that accompanies family life. The busy, active nature of what drove our schedules and demanded our attention on the home front proved to be the calm amidst our very storm. Ear infections, nebulizers, potty training, and preschool became the unlikely salve I used to dress our wounds and heal our hearts. There were urgent needs that demanded my attention leaving no time for thinking, wondering or dreaming.

Faith Filling

I was on a mission, even if Kevin wasn't. I wanted to go to church and he wasn't having any of it.

"What for?" he asked.

"Just because...let's go. Let's go to 'New Hope' right up the road, c'mon," I said.

"No hope," he'd say sarcastically and shut me down.

I was relentless and needed to receive all things positive and hopeful; bring on the heavenly blessings. A friend of mine was a regular at New Hope Hilo and invited me to join her at services, but I never felt moved to go, until now. I started and attended by myself, then I'd take Jonah, just a baby then, and we'd sit in the privacy of the nursing room tucked away in the back as I listened in on the live service. Ian came along and enjoyed all the new and unfamiliar toys contained in the adjacent playroom. Attending service was made so easy for parents and I felt so welcome and comfortable. I was also getting filled spiritually, like never, ever before.

Kevin was indignant and a little defiant; he just didn't want to go to church. He had strong Catholic roots, but really expressed little interest in giving God thanks for carrying him through brain surgery. On the other hand, I was so desperate for proof that God existed and that he was on my side. Meanwhile, Kevin carried a chip on his shoulder and went along with his daily tasks, while I pursued my newfound faith.

One Sunday, I packed up the boys and took them to service, and left Phoebe with Kevin watching a football game at home. Before I left, I asked them, "Do you want to come with us?" and they both shook their head to signal no. So I took a breath and went on my way. I remembered checking Ian in with the "Little Builders," toddler group and headed to the nursery with Jonah. I left Jonah there to play and made my way into the main sanctuary and sat with friends. This was new and liberating; it felt good to be able to sit with adults and listen to a sermon without the distraction of watching my kids. It also helped to know I'd be notified if either child had an accident or needed me.

At the end of the message, I felt a bump on my arm as my friend nudged me and pointed with her chin in the direction of where Kevin and Phoebe sat in the back. At first, I was stunned to see them there, then my surprise turned to elation! There way, way in the back row, sat my daughter and husband, with his only beanie covering his scarred head.

I tried not to overreact and make a big deal of it, in hopes that if I played it cool, he'd come again. But I couldn't help myself, then later I asked him, *why?* "What made you decide to come up to church?"

He said, "I felt bad. I looked at Phoebe after you left the house, and asked her, 'so do you want to go, or what?'" And she said, "Yeah, let's go, dad." "So we got ready and headed up," he said.

I am so thankful for Phoebe's words, urging Kevin to join the rest of us.

New Hope Hilo became our home church, where we established roots and flourished. New Hope Hilo's congregation became part of a precious extended faith-filled family.

Routine Day Trips

Kevin often flew to Oahu by himself to take his follow up MRIs at Queen's Medical Center regularly every few months. Day trips sometimes included a consult with his neurosurgeon immediately after to review MRI results. If he was unable to schedule a same-day appointment with his doctor, he'd immediately return to the airport and fly home. It became a familiar routine as I dropped him off at the airport and observed passengers who carried large hospital envelopes containing films, on their way to meet with doctors on Oahu. Many of the same folks would be on the return flight with Kevin, again, with their big envelopes in hand and personal stories held within.

By that time I was employed in town and no longer commuted long distances to work. My hour-long drive was replaced with a ten-minute skip and a hop to the nearby University of Hawaii at Hilo Campus. I was hired as a development officer for the University of Hawaii Foundation and excited about my brand new role as a fundraiser. It was entirely different from anything I'd done in my past. I was especially thankful for this new opportunity and the support I received from my new boss. Margaret took a chance on me and was supportive of the work and home fronts. She was aware of the frequent trips that Kevin was required to go on as we vigilantly monitored his health.

She leaned her head into my office one day during a planned day trip and gently asked if I had heard from Kevin yet. I remembered sitting behind my desk and looking up at her, while I shook my head, and struggled to hold back tears. "No, I haven't. Listen, Margaret, I'm sorry, but I'm going to shut my door now and try to call him," I said as I stood up from my chair and walked towards her. She nodded, gave me a reassuring smile and returned to her office.

Kevin knew how anxious I was during these trips and would call me immediately after he had a consult with his doctor. The fact that it was late afternoon and I had not heard from him yet, told me something was wrong. I dialed and heard him pick up his cell phone and it sounded loud and chaotic on the other end. The noisy background was unexpected and I scowled and asked, "Where are you?"

"I'm at Dave & Buster's with my sister having lunch," he said.

This wasn't unusual since his youngest sister Jennifer lived on Oahu. She was pursuing a second college degree and would meet up with Kevin during his trips and offer him rides whenever possible.

"Ok. So how was the appointment?" I asked.

He paused and said he'd call me later. I refused to be put off any longer and insisted he find a place to talk. I felt guilty for asking him with his sister listening in. *But, how dare he make me wait any longer?!*

"They said something showed up on the MRI. I'll call you later," he said.

I hung up without saying goodbye. I felt this painful emotional stab to the heart and I remembered crying softly at my desk. Next, Margaret stepped into my office, shut the door, sat down and hugged me as I cried into her shoulder.

So, shortly after we celebrated Jonah's first birthday, we learned that Kevin would need brain surgery number two.

Get Lost!

A tumor returned to the same location where the first one tried to set up residence in Kevin's left frontal lobe. I wanted to go back to the nice old Chinese uncle-like surgeon and call him out as a *liar!* He said the tumor was completely removed, so why was it back? I know, it wasn't his fault, but I wanted to point my finger and channel all that resentment and blame toward something, or someone. I wanted to hurt someone, an act of selfish revenge to inflict hurt like I was being hurt.

But by that time, the surgeon retired and Kevin was being seen by a new young neurosurgeon.

Again, I faced a situation that was out of my control and this angered me big time. I felt weak and disadvantaged, and mad! Yet, I also felt equally determined to be strong and support Kevin with everything I had. I walked into our first appointment with our new neurosurgeon packing some serious heat in the form of two pages of typewritten, single-spaced questions for him. I wanted answers, I wanted to understand what we were up against, I wanted options, I wanted someone we could trust and most of all, I wanted to hope. Dr. Morita delivered.

Kevin insisted that the doctor's eyes popped when he saw my list of questions. But I think my husband was hugely exaggerating. Indeed, the doc was genuinely patient and gracious as he respectfully listened and answered questions in a way we could understand. Make no mistake, he was direct and serious and surfaced complex questions that required big decisions. He asked, "During the surgery, if pathology reports show the tumor is more aggressive, do you want a Gliadel Wafer inserted into the resection cavity?" I shuddered and thought, *what do you mean? Chemo? Why, what for? Can't you just cut it out again and be done with it?*

Dr. Morita was a good doctor, a kind man, and someone I hated to see. He understood this.

Dejavu

Kevin had brain surgery number two in December 2006.
"How do you pronounce it again?" I asked. Dr. Morita explained the type and grade of the tumor based on the pathology report. I understood that the tumor cells were more aggressive than the first tumor and I tried hard not to go crazy. I looked nervously at Kevin, and he didn't look back. He was fixed on the doctor's words and the visit began to take on a serious downer vibe.

"I think that was what my kid sister had," I blurted.

Dr. Morita brushed my comment aside. I felt a little sting, and his words continued to linger in my head and bother me. So I waited impatiently for another pause and said again, I believe my half-sister had that same type of tumor. I explained it was fatal and she died shortly after she celebrated her 9th birthday. She passed more than a decade earlier in 1995. It was a sensitive story because it involved my half-sister, born out of wedlock and introduced to siblings shortly before her death.

She was sixteen years younger than me and lived on Oahu with her mother. I developed a relationship with her, and while I attended college on Oahu, we'd hang out on occasion. I enjoyed an "aunty" role and wanted to make sure her home life was as stable as possible.

I also loved my three half-siblings living on the Big Island, who had no idea that another half-sister existed until she was terminally ill. Shortly before she died, she received her wish to meet her sister and two brothers here in Hilo. We met up at Ken's House of Pancakes for lunch. My memory of that visit was that it was awkward, tender, uncomfortable, and altogether bittersweet.

Kevin was aware of my sister who died from a brain tumor, but we never made a big deal about it. Admittedly, it was strange that I have had two loved ones with brain tumors, yet I honestly didn't dwell on that or think much of it. When Mindy was diagnosed, I remembered her tumor to be the worse one out there and it was sizable, so she flew to the University of California San Francisco (UCSF) for the best treatments available. At that time I returned to Hilo after finishing college and wasn't present to experience her decline. We kept in touch by phone and I flew over to spend time with her before she passed.

I told Dr. Morita that my sister was a patient at UCSF many years earlier and was treated with Gamma-knife radiation. I told him she had that horrible brain cancer; I don't want Kevin to have that same one I thought. Dr. Morita looked at me and asked, "What was her name? Your sister, what was your sister's name?" I took a quick breath and slowly responded "Mindy," and, he finished and said her last name.

Gasp!

Chicken skin swept over my entire body from head to toe as I tried to process how he knew that. My eyes teared as I looked to Kevin in disbelief. *"What? How?"* I muttered. All Kevin could say was "wow, wow" and shook his head side to side.

Dr. Morita said he knew Mindy as a patient at UCSF; he was something like the designated Resident in Charge of the pediatric neurosurgery then. *Seriously? You knew her and now you're taking care of my husband? What are the chances?*

I asked Dr. Morita, "How can you not be as shocked about this as we are?"

He spoke calmly and said something about how this community of brain tumor patients is often very small, and it's not too surprising when people and experiences overlap. Well, overlapping experiences is an understatement, because here was a doctor who bridged brain tumor experiences between two people in my life. Eleven years earlier he met and treated my half-sister as a patient, and later, my husband was under his care. How strange. I didn't know what to make of it and tried hard not to make too much out of it either. Years into the future, there would be many more patients and physicians we shared in common with overlapping stories.

Wake Up Call

The second surgery was a huge wake-up call for Kevin and me. We learned that the tumor was more aggressive. The earlier tumor was a grade two, and now it was a grade three. Kevin was forced to consider the recommended radiation as soon as he regained strength, followed by chemotherapy. We expected a very rough road ahead because treatment descriptions were new and unfamiliar to us, and the expenses were starting to add up. The kids were ages five, two and one at the time.

Kevin wasn't invincible and bravely channeled his energy in preparation for the treatments ahead. He decided to see a radiation oncologist on Oahu, which required him to remain on Oahu for treatments for a couple of months. He'd have to stay at the same apartment complex that I stayed at while he was a hospital patient; available for out-of-town patients and families to rent. It was extremely convenient for Kevin to be able to walk to his daily radiation treatments at Queen's and return to the unit to rest when he was done. I struggled because as much as I wanted to support his decision to be cared for by the doctor of his choice, we'd be sacrificing on other fronts, like family time, interaction and overall presence and support. I hated the sacrifice, the circumstances, all of it!

I began to stress about our finances and thought it would be so much easier for him to go through treatments locally. He could see a local doctor on the island and we wouldn't have the added rental expense. But Kevin established a relationship with his radiation oncologist and this kind of trust was crucial and could not be compromised. He was preparing for battle, and he needed a physician who would be armored with technology, information, skills, and compassion. I knew this in my heart and how much I needed to support this choice, buck up, be positive, and believe that Kevin was making the best decision for his health and our family.

Kevin was unable to return to work as he did after his first surgery and as a sole proprietor and family breadwinner, our family income decreased significantly. No work meant no income. Kevin's business account reserves sustained us and allowed us to pay our bills as we figured out how to transition from two incomes to a single-income family. We immediately sought information on social security benefits and received approval from Queen's to be put on a special payment plan. We were stable.

Later, as our financial reserves began to dry up, we learned that Kevin's entire lodging bill was paid anonymously. We never received a bill but estimated we owed thousands of dollars for more than six weeks of a one-bedroom rental. This was such an enormous financial burden that melted away before our very eyes and we didn't need to deal with at all. We were so humbled by someone's generosity and deeply grateful. We never found out who picked up Kevin's lodging tab but will forever be grateful for their kindness.

Home Away From Home

For nearly two months Kevin faithfully marched to his daily radiation treatments, which lasted all of twenty minutes per session; that was the easy part. The hard part was filling in the time during the rest of the day. He sometimes roamed around the hospital and occasionally walked over to the public library next door across the street. He was lonely and during our nightly phone calls, I heard all about his transient neighbors and looked forward to hearing about the meals that his Aunt Betty brought over.

Aunt Betty, Kevin's step-dad's sister, was a maternal angel. Kevin lost his mom several years earlier and appreciated his relationship with Aunt Betty. She was amazing and stepped in to help with providing meals for Kevin during his extended time on Oahu. One week, Kevin was especially excited when he told me that Aunt Betty brought over a stack of steaks. I was confused and clarified, "a steak?" He said, "no, a stack of cooked steaks." I said, "really? I hope you have enough rice to go with that big stack of steaks." He said he had enough for the week and planned to share it with his sisters Jennifer and Cindy who visited him frequently as well. He also had a very steady supply of homemade chocolate chip cookies.

While at Queen's, Kevin amassed a collection of model cars that he worked on while watching tons of TV reruns during the day. He asked the kids for their input on colors to paint the finished models. Aside from building models, he was responsible for countless hours of TV viewing. I knew all the characters of the Grays Anatomy series without watching a single episode, ever. Kevin recapped seasons worth of the TV series over our nightly telephone calls. It's true and I'm not proud of it.

Fridays would slowly roll around and if his blood counts were stable, he was allowed to fly home and spend the weekend with us. If everything went well, I would receive a call giving me a head's up sometime mid-morning and look forward to picking him up in the afternoon.

Air travel was costly and we would not have been able to afford Kevin's frequent flights back and forth, if not for the thousands of donated miles we received. Throughout his radiation treatment, he flew an estimated ten round trips between the Big Island and Oahu. Friends and family shared precious miles with us, which allowed us to book Kevin's flights.

We were cautiously optimistic because we were well aware of the elevated exposure to germs, while Kevin's immune system became weaker and weaker. He could've, should've remained in one location to minimize germ exposure, rather than travel on an airplane. But I was selfish and wanted him home with us. I couldn't stand that the connection between Kevin and the kids was limited to a phone call. I wanted him near. I wanted the kids to know that their dad loved them, and for him to be nearby to express his love in person. This was important to me, and he flew home as much as possible, despite the germs.

Weekend Cruiser

Phoebe always asked when her dad would come home next and I'd have to remind her we needed to wait for the weekend. We all hated the wait, me most of all. Nights were horrible as I tried to deflect this subtle sense of fear as it tried to sneak in and snuggle with us. I fought hard against this fear and would corral the kids into the boys' bedroom each night where we'd all sleep together. I convinced Phoebe to join me in the boy's room; it would be fun, like camping. I'd play it up and take out every sleeping bag and comforter we owned and made a big deal as I laid them on the ground between the crib and bed. "*See, just like camping, right?*" I fluffed the blankets and tossed a few extra pillows into the mix for fun. It looked like a big messy rodent nest on the floor, but for me, this was my power cave, where I felt safe and secure.

When Kevin was home, he would *cruise*. Kevin was tired and would sleep a lot, especially midway through his radiation treatment. But the kids enjoyed having him home and accepted this routine as normal. They didn't realize that their dad was pooped and couldn't help but *tap out* for long periods during the day. He would sometimes wave to us from the kitchen window, as we played downstairs on the street. Life was simple, time was spent leisurely, and I remembered how happy I felt when Kevin had enough energy to come downstairs and sit with me on the sidewalk. There in comfortable silence, we'd watch the kids whirring past us with their bikes and trike. We were present, watching them together and I was thankful.

One weekend, Phoebe was on a mission and determined to help her class win a prize for collecting the most telephone books at school. She was five or six at the time and I made up a bunch of excuses for why I couldn't accompany her. I wasn't out to win *Mom of the Year* recognition. In fact, I could rattle off so many other mom-things I had to do first. Sure, I felt a little guilty, but not enough to break down and go with her and knock on doors to ask for phone books.

Kevin must have overheard my excuses, or maybe Phoebe went behind my back to work on her dad, who knows. But there he stood on our road, with his charcoal gray beanie covering his bald scarred head. He walked alongside Phoebe while toting the big red Little Tykes plastic wagon. I cried as I watched them from the window; my husband, showing me up and demonstrating to his daughter that he would support her no matter what, even if it required collecting old phone books. They came back with heaps and I don't even know if her class won. It didn't matter, because Phoebe learned on the inside what it meant to be a winner.

House Dads Are Cool

Chemotherapy followed radiation and lasted nearly a year. Treatment after treatment wiped my husband out. He was beyond spent and unable to return to his self-employed schedule as a mobile mechanic. This was tough for him as he went from being the family's breadwinner to collecting social security and taking on the role of house dad. Although harmful to his man-pride at first, this extended period ended up being powerful and precious! He went from putting in mega hours of hard physical labor to being gaunt, weak and pale from avoiding time in the sun. He spent time regaining his strength while at home and bonded with the kids.

Our roles evolved, and as I went to work, he was increasingly present for the kids at home and after school. During Phoebe and Ian's elementary years, he'd volunteer to chaperone for every field trip and was deeply satisfied when teachers assigned him to watch over the class rascals. The ugly green monster would sometimes surface in me if I let it, whenever the kids would recount their days with dad, or when Kevin would rattle off names of classmates. I could barely keep up with the names of their current teachers and would have to remind myself to energize the corners of my mouth to grin as envy fought to expose my jealousy. Why was I so bothered by this? Well because involved parents were cool, and our kids had a very cool parent, it just wasn't me.

I tried to meet up and attend school assemblies as much as possible, but it was my husband who was present without fail. He was able to arrive early and stake out premium seats for late arrivals like me. He also helped with the bulk of afterschool logistics shuttling kids to- and from-school, t-ball, and tennis, soccer, etc. He also earned "Parent Volunteer" of the year recognition for consecutive years and had a collection of badges he earned with hours tallied riding the big yellow school bus for field trips to the local fire department, the zoo, and parks.

On the domestic front, Kevin helped with everything from laundry, meal prep and even experimented with bread-baking. I know he didn't enjoy being at home full time, but he acknowledged the need to take the time to recover and stepped up with meeting a different form of family needs. Only through reflection, am I able to fully appreciate how his presence at home eased stress in a big way. It was simple things like having clean clothes, washed, folded, and put away for a new day at school and work. It was having the dinner meal prepared by the time we were all united at home. It was opening the refrigerator and having it filled with groceries. It was having the kids' homework completed and put away.

Prior to Kevin being at home, it felt like we were in a constant state of frenzy. He'd work from sun up and past sundown and the sound of his diesel work truck could be heard coming down our street, signaling to the kids that dad was home. One time, I remembered how short-tempered I was while I stood at the kitchen sink washing the rice pot and Kevin reversed his truck into his parking space. It was late, the kids had to be fed, and there was nothing thawed out to cook. Then I heard Kevin turn off his engine and Phoebe stood on the couch and happily yelled out the window, "Hi dad, mom is making SPAM and beans for dinner again!" Before I could quiet him, the whole neighborhood knew our gourmet dinner plans. *Oh great.* But that kind of haste, tension and frustration was the norm before we had Kevin at home full-time. He was the special glue that made our family strong and secure while he spurred our developing faith.

Storing Our Treasures

Finances were lean during years when Kevin was unemployed, but we were never lacking in any kind of provision. Kevin qualified for social security benefits and we managed. The kids were fed, mortgage and hospital bills paid, household utilities enjoyed, and two pet dogs cared for; life was full and good. Most importantly, there was the added benefit of having a parent at home. Simply being present and around to listen, to talk, to help with homework, to watch t-ball practices; all of it priceless.

It was also a crucial time for Kevin to be able to recover from his extended chemotherapy treatment. He went from being the dedicated workhorse, capable of working in the most grueling conditions, during long hours without complaining. He was all about constant productivity and was deeply satisfied when others appreciated his work ethic. All in a day's work, grease and grime mindset no longer translated to a paycheck and he directed his efforts towards being resourceful.

Kevin always paid attention to sales, but he became a super savvy shopper and trained our kids on the craft of coupon shopping. They were familiar with the term "maximum limit," mastered tearing out coupons from the newspaper while standing in the check out line, and, knew where to find spare ones in the grocery stores in case it was needed. He also baked bread and prepared sandwiches for work and school lunches. A few times, he even harvested tomatoes from the garden and created his version of tomato sauce, complete with seeds.

There were also mini "jobs" that began to pop up now and again. Neighbors and friends began to bring over their chain saws, weed whackers, and riding lawn mowers to fix. It seemed like everyone had something small that needed to be looked at and fixed, and a list of projects always seemed to occupy Kevin's time. This, that, and the other earned him free golf ball buckets at the driving range, loaves of banana bread, fish, and food in trade. Life was full of blessings that came in different ways and forms.

Got Activities?

Kevin said, "We need something for Ian to do. We've given so much attention to Phoebe and now we should let Ian try something for himself."

He had a point. Phoebe had dabbled in gymnastics, hula, soccer, and golf, and she was just seven years old.

"What do you have in mind?" I asked.

"Maybe t-ball. The church league just started up again. I'll take him to the field to watch them practice," he said.

"Are we ready for this?" I asked. In my mind, I fought the urge to keep life simple and avoid added responsibilities.

"Why not?" he responded.

Fair enough, I thought. Kevin's feeling good, he's healthy and whole. We'll give it a shot and see what Ian makes of it. Well, Ian seemed to tolerate it, but it ended up being Phoebe who loved the game of baseball.

We spent ten years in this youth sports world and experienced the full spectrum from preschool-aged t-ball to high school baseball and softball. Kevin joined the kids on the field and volunteered to help in their early years as a coach. He thrived being involved and often participated in their practices. Kevin has always been intensely proud of his kids and throws himself 100 percent behind nearly anything and everything they do. He was a borderline fanatic and it used to drive me nuts when he and Phoebe would have a post-game analysis of her softball games. No one could penetrate that discussion space and he would attempt to counsel as she re-lived plays, complained about missed opportunities, or punish herself for mistakes made during a game. Something he was better at than I was. My approach was, have fun, get over it, and move on.

As the kids advanced in levels and moved to different teams, we established meaningful friendships, encountered all kinds of drama and spent countless hours at the ballpark. It was a huge investment of time, energy and resources. We were all in as parent supporters, and Phoebe and Ian both enjoyed and excelled in this space for a while. They later decided to pivot during their freshman years in high school and traded in their bats and gloves. Phoebe dedicated two years to Junior Achievement business basics and Ian swapped clunky baseball cleats for featherweight running track shoes.

Jonah was our very welcome anomaly. He decided early on that baseball wasn't his thing. He broke out of the sibling's baseball shadow and eventually turned his attention to robotics. This allowed us to experience something entirely new and exciting, and, remain indoors for a change. We learned about robot leagues, "challenges" and witnessed the building and coding of these robot creations from scratch. We were so impressed with the design and function of the robots, then fascinated to watch as students used their technical skills to operate their bots, perform specific functions and strategically earn points to win. Kevin was easily lured into this scene and always had advice on hand to offer Jonah. He donated upgraded and spare parts to the program so that they could be used in the ongoing refining efforts of their robot build-outs. Again, all in!

Return To Work

During nearly four years, Kevin regained body strength and built up endurance. Eventually, he felt strong enough and was physically ready to return to work. He wanted to go back to work. I was apprehensive and fought back this unease of what "work" would be like for him, and more importantly, what that would mean for our family.

Self-employment was not an ideal option and I worked hard to convince my husband to take a different approach to return to work. I insisted that work-place benefits were critically important to us. I know how much he loved the autonomy and ability to schedule his projects, but this freedom came with a cost. I was focused on stability; applying to a local company that would provide health insurance, paid vacation, and retirement options. The financial risk of being self-employed was too great, especially since we had become a family of five.

Kevin was hired immediately after he put his feelers out into the work universe. As a result, our family activities and priorities shifted again. He felt strong and adjusted quickly to the rigor of physically working full-time hours as a mechanic. He was officially an employee, and I was grateful for the covered benefits and the employer's flexibility in accommodating his medical appointments.

Science VS. Screws

While the kids were still young, something sinister reared its head in an MRI, again.

I hunkered down. *We've come so far* I thought to myself. Our family was together and we enjoyed stability for several years. I was also thankful that the kids were mostly oblivious to the past cancer diagnosis, surgeries, and treatment because they were so young. Their reality was simple and having dad at home was a part of it.

So I was forced to put my *warrior wife* hat on again. Dr. Morita assured us that the recommended procedure was "non-invasive." My understanding was that it was a highly targeted radiation therapy done at a specialized facility on Oahu. The time required was minimal and we would even be able to fly home that same day. This seemed almost too manageable and I held my breath as we proceeded with caution.

Although it was one day, it took a tremendous amount of energy to prepare psychologically. *"How would this be different from other treatments? How will Kevin be impacted? What can we expect after the procedure?"* I wondered. Well, it was quite different and not as I expected.

We flew to Oahu early in the morning and found our way to the medical center well ahead of time. The most difficult part of this experience was observing the nurses getting Kevin ready for the procedure. I had to breathe deeply and remind myself to remain calm and smile at Kevin while nurses screwed metal-looking posts into his skull to stabilize his head. The nurses explained that this was necessary to prevent movement during the procedure. Honestly, I was beyond relieved when they wheeled my husband away, and I could exhale all that pent up brave-face façade! A couple of hours later, he returned, looking and seeming okay. I was amazed.

We arrived at the airport at home in the late afternoon. As we drove home, he looked at me with two dinky band-aids covering up the spots where the screw marks remained and told me he wanted to meet Phoebe at the evening science activity at school. *"What?!"* I looked at my husband incredulously. In my mind, I said to myself, *Look, I get it…it was a long day for you. Well, guess what?! It was a long day for me too.*

Seriously frustrated, I explained to Kevin that my mom was there with Phoebe and all was well; she was fine and wasn't suffering because we weren't there to support her. He was not listening. "I want to go. I want to see what they're doing. Just drop me off, I'll be fine," he said. I was tired and wanted to go home. I did not feel like putting on a happy face and going to the school cafeteria where we'd be expected to engage with teachers and parents. *No thanks!* I struggled and asked myself *how could I let him go, he just went through a gamma knife radiation procedure for goodness sake?!*

Well, I relented and dropped him off at the school cafeteria, then made my way home. My mom dropped Kevin and Phoebe off at home after the event. That was Kevin, the stubborn husband, supportive dad, and big kid who wanted to play science. They came home with a brush bot made from a toothbrush, complete with a tiny motor.

Sigh.

Youtube + Home Depot = Boy Genius

Technology is shaping our world and the future generation in crazy ways. Kids today have access to news, ideas, and information like never before. Gone are the days when kids like me stayed home during school breaks and watched movies on HBO and talked on the phone for hours; too boring for kids today.

The realities for youth are markedly different from my own experiences and I'm troubled by the influences that continue to shape it. I've observed my kids along with their network of "real friends" and "computer friends," convene over the Internet to form teams where they make pretend and can virtually participate in combat computer games where they can kill and destroy without flinching.

Even in the middle of the Pacific, access to the worldwide web allows us to enjoy the benefits of Amazon.com and YouTube, along with the ugly and less talked about stuff that requires vigilant monitoring as parents. Indeed, the world has been flattened where the same information is accessible; to be used for good, or bad, but available to all.

The transition between technology's overall role in growing up was most evident with Jonah. As a toddler, he was obsessed with heavy equipment machinery and delighted in the mail catalogs where he could recite every attachment ever created. We'd make him perform for friends and demonstrate his great wisdom and ability in distinguishing a bucket loader from an augur; he was three years old. A couple of years later his fascination with machinery lead him to a television show called Swamp Loggers. On his own, he'd search up old episodes on YouTube and contentedly watch reruns for hours. This was a prelude of sorts to understanding how much of a presence YouTube had in their lives.

As "tweens" both boys would work on plots to get their dad to take them shopping at Home Depot. They'd watch YouTube videos and talk incessantly about projects. One time, they insisted on building a laser blow dart gun with a scope. I blew off the crazy talk and tuned out, but not Kevin. His response was: *So what, where's your list? How are you going to build something without a parts list? Show me your design.*

Sometimes the boys would deliver. Scrawled lists of this and that would be compelling and give Kevin an excuse to go to Home Depot.

Ian was my biggest concern and scarily went through this obsession with knives, sharp edges in general, and took a liking to Ninja stars. He drew a design on graph paper once for his dad and can you guess what happened next? Yes, my husband obliged, cut the design out of metal, and, *voila*, I had a Filipino Ninja-wannabe in the house. We are talking metal and pointed. *Furious* came close to how I felt when Ian bolted out of the house one afternoon to show off his hand-crafted Ninja star to a visitor and demonstrated his throwing prowess. He dragged out an old wooden pallet, placed it against the side of the house where it made a loud "thwack!" sound when he threw the star and its blade made contact with the wood. Mad mom confiscated the star after it was pried from the pallet, and it hasn't seen daylight since.

Another time, it was a blow dart gun. *Why are you leading them to believe they can buy parts to build this thing anyway?* I found it impractical and costly to build a dart gun with PVC pipes and mini flashlights as a scope. That's what the Nerf guns were for, but they persisted. *What?! You need special camouflage duct tape to decorate it, too?* Again, this made no sense to me. But to Kevin, he was proud and told me the process was useful and insisted the project was creative.

That's how the boys rolled with their dad. Ian and Jonah each built their blow dart gun complete with camouflage duct tape and homemade paper darts to go with it.

Whatever.

Squealing

Special bonds between Kevin and the kids were evident because of their concentrated time together when they were younger. Even as teenagers, though they are older and bolder, the dinner table stories of "remember when" reveal a sacred closeness between them. Recollections start off playful and end with a lot of "squealing."

"Dad, I remember when you used to pick us up after school. When we got home, you let us watch TV while you napped on your comfy chair," Phoebe said.

"What?! No, I wasn't napping!" Kevin snapped back.

"Yeah right…and then we would sneak downstairs to ride our bikes while you were sleeping," Ian said.

"I wasn't sleeping; I told you I was resting my eyes," Kevin insisted.

Jonah said, *"I remember dad taking us to McDonald's after school, and told us not to tell mom."*

They still do this.

Bike Booboo

Home life was steady and seemed normal for several years.

One weekend, it was late in the afternoon and I held a load of laundry beneath my right arm. I was on my way downstairs to the laundry room when I stepped into my slippers and started down the landing onto the stairs. As I looked up, I gasped and stopped to take in the scene, and then I couldn't move. Before I go any further, I'll have to take you back a week in time.

Ian and Jonah had been building a bike ramp, resourcefully piecing old plywood around the house, angled against some dirt beneath it to create the incline. Their project occupied a good portion of our cemented driveway area and seemed harmless enough. It kept them out of the house and burned a lot of energy. I could hear them take turns as they rode their bikes down the street at full speed, pedal up the ramp and sort of catch some air. It was fun to peek out and watch them from build-out to ride. Kevin mostly encouraged their projects until he took over and wanted in on the action.

Back to the laundry... I remembered heading downstairs with a load of dirty laundry under my arm and I stopped mid-stairs. I shook my head in disbelief and watched my husband riding one of the bikes. There he was, pumping the pedals like crazy, trying to work up his speed as he headed for the ramp at the edge of the driveway. I couldn't move and the distance between Kevin and the ramp was decreasing quickly. *What was he thinking?!*

I couldn't believe he'd attempt to jump off this kiddie ramp. I didn't want to watch, yet my eyes were locked on him and unable to turn away. Then finally, Kevin's senses caught up with him, but it was too late. He screeched and his hand brakes made a shrill piercing noise as the tires skidded. And in verrrrry sloooooow motion, I saw the rear bike tire lift up and flip over the front tire, which flew Kevin, the man-kid to the ground with a heavy soundless **THUD!**

I heard laughter and Jonah said, "Wow, that was the funniest thing I saw in my life!" Kevin stood up slowly, looked at the boys on the road, then made eye contact with me and laughed too. He picked up the bike then walked and retreated to the garage, out of sight. The boys both looked to see what I would do. Well, my shock and concern turned to some ugly words and each of the kids has a different version of what I said exactly.

Ian caught up with Kevin downstairs and I heard him say, "Dad, you're bleeding!" That was it, I heard enough. I took my angry face, mean words and stomped back upstairs with my dirty laundry. I was so mad and accused him of being a "stupid old man" for doing something foolish like attempting to take his man-framed body down the street on the tiny bike to face the kid ramp. Then he ended up at the very last second, coming to his senses and chickened out. "*What were you thinking?*" I screamed in my head. I realized quickly enough he was not thinking!

Now he had more battle scars, this time they were on his knees.

Phoebe (3) and Ian (six months) during Christmas. (December 2004)

Andrea Furuli

Phoebe (4) and Jonah (newborn). (October 2005)

Kevin and Phoebe take on a game of chess.

Andrea Furuli

Furuli boys are bound for the beach.

Kevin, Phoebe and Ian hang out between games at
one of many, many baseball tournaments.

Family enjoys the panoramic view at Oahu's
Diamond Head lookout. (2014)

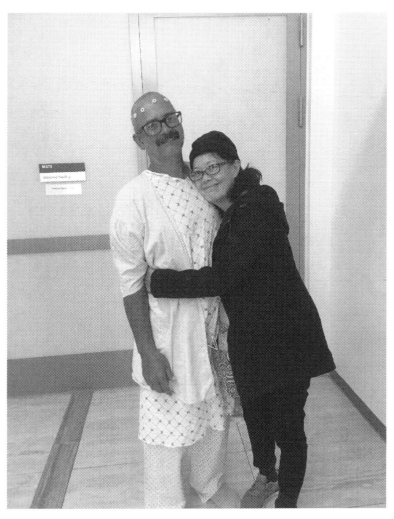

Kevin and Andrea "ready up" as he prepares for
his 4th brain surgery. (February 2019)

Andrea Furuli

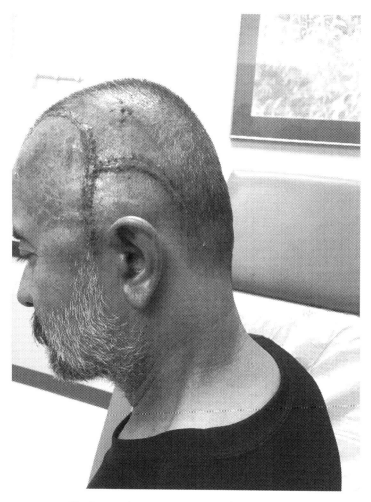

Kevin gets his sutures removed. (Feb. 2019)

Family throws Phoebe a high school graduation party. (June 2019)

Kevin takes in his personal definition of "success" to help his kids find their way….Phoebe receives dad escort to George Fox University. (August 2019)

They Know

Shielding the kids from scary and ugly things was always a priority. Eventually, I realized my efforts were only partly effective at best, and the kids absorbed more than I thought. They made sense of our circumstances, all the while, and coped in their own way.

Kevin once returned from a trip to Oahu for an MRI and check-up. He walked in during dinner and Ian, 5 or 6 at the time, looked up and said, "Oh, hi dad, how was your brain picture?" It was jarring for me to hear him ask, and I thought *what do you know about dad's 'brain pictures?'* I felt like I failed from protecting my child from knowing about the threat of cancer possibly returning. But awareness penetrated his kid psyche in small doses over the years; in fact, they were all aware and had been impacted in their own way.

Jonah, too, surprised me when he came to my bedroom one night before bed. As a little squirt in the second or third grade, he climbed on to the bed to watch TV with me. He lay his head down on Kevin's pillow then he shot straight up and touched his head. He looked at Kevin's pillow and asked me whether he was going to "catch it," referring to his dad's illness. I quickly diffused his worry and assured him that "it" was not contagious. I was relieved that Kevin wasn't around to hear any of that.

The biggest heartache experienced was with Phoebe in the seventh grade. I remembered checking her grades online and discovered she had multiple Fs. This blew my mind and was a serious *say what* moment for me as a mom. Stunned and convinced that I was played by my own teenager; I was one angry mom when I reached out and spoke with her counselor. I started with a big attitude and demanded answers to why teachers had not bothered to notice that my daughter went from As to Fs and didn't bother to call me. I had a big portion of blame to dish out and yet I was totally unprepared for the follow-up call I received.

The counselor met with Phoebe and explained that my daughter was deeply affected by what was going on at home. She was aware that cancer had returned evidenced by the growth in Kevin's MRI and described to the counselor how I had been researching clinical trials online for her dad. She was scared and told her counselor that she had to be brave in front of her brothers because they looked up to her. It was so true; her bros looked up to her a lot. My heart broke.

Awareness capped with fear and anxiety was a heavy burden for me to carry, but the realization that Phoebe also carried this weight crushed me. I was oblivious to how my actions were being observed and regretted that it took me so long to figure out. I thought I was successfully protecting my kids from fear, mortality and the junk that happens in life. I believed I was doing the right thing then understood that hiding bad and ugly things were harmful, for my kids and me. We had our first official "this is where we're at" family meeting.

It was a Saturday afternoon and the boys were getting ready to be picked up by my sister for a sleepover with their cousin Tobey. After years of vigilant monitoring, we braced after we received news that there was some "color enhancement" that showed up on an MRI. I insisted that we needed to talk with the kids after we put it off much too long. There we all sat together on the living room sofas. It was stuffy and the boys were antsy. Kevin started to talk, then stopped. He couldn't continue and looked over at me and nodded as he said: "You go." That was my cue.

"Guys, dad's doctor told us that there was something on his last MRI. They think it's cancer," I said as my lips quivered and warm tears rolled down my cheeks. The kids were uncomfortable and looked around at each other. Kevin picked up the dialogue and said something like "I'm not dying. But you guys need to know because we all need to be strong." Phoebe began to cry. Ian tried hard to be stoic but soon burst and became emotional. He stood up to find a tissue box. Jonah took everything in and neither cried or asked questions, but sat there without showing much emotion at all. I talked about cancer and described it as a sickness and that dad was going to have to work hard at staying healthy to fight cancer.

"Does anyone want to ask a question?" I asked them.

No response.

My sister arrived in our driveway and the boys couldn't jump up and exit the house fast enough. I originally felt as though this was an imposition by my sister, to interrupt this critical family discussion. But I quickly realized how it was more like a divine invitation for Ian and Jonah. We just delivered a horrible dose of reality and kids were resilient, picked it up, threw it in the air and mentally kicked it hard before moving on. I ended up being grateful for the distraction.

Just Hang On

During most of the tween to teen years, Kevin had been on chemotherapy. Most people apart from my closest friends and innermost circles had any idea that a brain tumor threat persisted. My husband endured several years of continuous chemotherapy in a valiant attempt to keep it controlled. Few people ever knew.

We were connected with a Neuro Oncologist at UCSF by this time. This came as a result of Kevin's longtime neurosurgeon in Hawaii, who explained that his then-current MRI revealed a likely tumor growth, but described it as inoperable. We pursued a second opinion and the UCSF doctor we were consulting with conferred with the Neurosurgeon; surgery was offered as an option. However, Kevin chose chemotherapy to avoid the risks of an operation.

It was grueling for him and included some of the same drugs that he took before, like CCNU and Temodar. There was a new medication (to us) called Avastin, and we were hopeful, so hopeful that Avastin would be "the one" to kick butt. A couple of years of ongoing chemo made him sick and nauseous. He never ever complained.

Powerless on the sidelines, I braced for the chemo cycles and prayed for Kevin to get through. On severe nights, Kevin would rush to the bathroom to vomit then early in the morning, somehow, he'd manage to pull himself together and find the will to go to work. The cycles wore him down and he was noticeably fatigued, and yet missed work, maybe twice.

My husband was strong, but I think he was getting tired of being strong.

"All I want is to watch the kids grow up and to see what they become," Kevin would tell me over and over again. He said, "I wonder if they'll remain close when they grow up?" By this time, Kevin was in his early fifties and I was in my late forties, and our adult lives had been focused on stabilizing Kevin's health while responding to and reinforcing whatever was going on in the kids' lives.

Time doesn't stand still and the world keeps spinning. Life buzzes on at home with family, within personal circles, and at work with colleagues. No matter what was going on, there seems to have always been a continuous force that compelled us to keep going...the kids had homework to do, fundraiser car wash tickets to sell, potluck dishes to prepare, laundry to fold, groceries to buy, blood tests to take, MRIs to schedule; life was constantly spinning around us.

In a moment of reflection, I can understand how folks really wouldn't know what was going on beneath the surface of my life. My family appeared intact and reasonably normal for any outsider looking in. Kevin dropped off and picked up kids from practices, attended games, had a job, drove his truck, and bantered with other parents. The kids had their peers, managed school responsibilities and plugged into their daily reality. As for me, I maintained my work responsibilities and as a family, together we enjoyed stay-cations, attended tournaments, and went to church service on Sundays. How could anyone fighting cancer and on chemotherapy for so long be doing this?

It wasn't easy. Our family fought hard, whether we realized it or not, and no one worked harder than Kevin to be present and alive, well and whole.

Who Needs Disney?

Some families enjoyed vacations that took them to Honolulu and Disney Land, or to far-off destinations to visit family and friends. I often envied hearing about the travel adventures that other families experienced and resented that we were nowhere near being able to afford such a luxury. Our lives were centered on being grateful for what we had and living simply and within our means.

Family adventures paired us with friends with whom we were blessed to enjoy island adventures that took us to beautiful, breathtaking, and hidden from most of the world kind of locations right here in our backyard. Our families picked seasonal fruit in Keanakolu, swam with turtles at Punalu`u, perfected S'mores on the campfire and basked in the tidepools at Kapoho. Walter took us along with his family to expose us to some unique places literally from the mountain to the ocean where kids and adults bonded over starry skies, and hot cocoa, to admiring turtles basking on the black sand beaches in the south. We spent hours contentedly playing board games, talking story and snacking non-stop. I cannot express the depth of gratitude I have for the friends and memories etched on my mind and heart for the many, many, trips we've enjoyed with our extended family.

The kids loved our camping trips. But still, they occasionally spoke of classmates and others they knew who went on vacations to places like Disney Land. I'd try my best to squash the jealousy that was trying to take root and insist anyone could go to Disney Land, but how many folks went camping at "Uncle Walter's Cabin," or glamping at timeshares in Kona? Roughing it at the mountain cabin or lazing at the pool was cool! Well, this satisfied their collective thirst for travel for a short while and eventually, the savings of stay-cations for a family of five paid off.

One year, we traded our designated timeshare for another location on a lake in Washington and had the most marvelous time at a choice location! We packed on to the trip extended visits with family in Victoria, British Columbia, and Washington and took in the beautiful scenery, friendly people and happy vibes in general. We had so much fun and worked hard to create this memory maker. Our first family vacation and the kids were 10, 12 and 15. Again, this was a big deal and took us years and years to save up for it.

Disney Land? We haven't made it to the most magical place on earth yet. "You can go when you have kids of your own," I told them.

Andrea Furuli

Framily

Many years ago, my friend Aimee prayed during one of our many family gatherings. As she blessed our food she called attention to everyone present and gave thanks to God for our friends and family, but what we all heard her say was, "thank you Lord for our **framily**." We all giggled, agreed in spirit, and that endearing term has stuck with our circle ever since.

Our framily means the world to us.

We've camped (they say "glamped") at the most beautiful and remote places on the Big Island

We've enjoyed the most over-the-top potlucks, complete with decadent desserts and enough leftovers to feed our families for a week after.

We've rested in the assurance that we are covered by friends who are willing to stand in the gap with us no matter what.

We've experienced tender losses and triumphs together.

We've laughed and cried, then laughed and cried some more, because we can.

We freely reach out, and lean on, anytime we feel like it or need to.

We all love our kids, and each other's kids even when we can't stand them.

We are who we are because of and thanks to our framily.

Hormones

Being a teenager is tough. Being a parent of a teenager is even tougher, I'm certain of this. There is no escaping hormones and the wonky everything that comes with it.

Thank you, God, for placing Kevin in this family for such a time as this - puberty. I am thankful for the times when big surly dad-Kevin pulled in to the parking lot to pick up Phoebe, and the man talk that helped address Ian's and Jonah's cracking voices, hair growth, and whatever else is attached to this time. Again, I am indebted to my husband because if not for his presence, I would have made like an ostrich and buried my head in the sand. Either that or likely lose it.

He was undoubtedly the glue that attached my daughter and I, like broken pieces of pottery, back together, when we were both indignant and could barely stand to be in the same room together. He'd also manage to communicate with boys when I just thought they were strange, selfish and punky creatures. There is no way that I'd be able to manage all the wayward craziness that comes with teenagers and be a kind and compassionate spouse too; no way. So in speaking truth, our very own family battles, although fierce at times, were part of what makes us close and strong.

This is where I find myself today, between appreciating the good days when I could still boss them around, compared to my desire to lock them all up in a "grow up room" where they will mature and turn into kind young adults. See, today the kids are a lot cockier and don't hold back in telling me how they feel either.

I've been accused of being mean and impatient and referred to as the fire-breathing-acid-spitting-dragon.

Hey, no offense taken, I'm just doing my job.

All in all, the kids are spicy, but solid and doing okay. Kevin's presence during this time is important and genuinely appreciated. He is the calm to my chaos, and the patience that melts my intolerance. This is not meant to put my husband on a pedestal, but my way of acknowledging that he has been the very source of pause and much-needed buffer when I feel myself on the edge with the kids. He too is harsh and strict at times, yet always, always keeps them accountable.

As for the trio, they've been exposed to dad's illness and experienced strength, perseverance, grace, compassion, and love. But let's be real, life is still H-A-R-D, and they get it. In fact, they know it intimately. So on top of hormones and everything else life throws their way, the kids have managed to figure out, for the most part, what's truly important.

Season of Uncertainty

No, Not Again!

Something ominous loomed over the start of the New Year. We'd soon ring in and welcome 2019, although a sense of foreboding hung heavily like humidity before a hurricane.

Six months earlier, my husband underwent an "awake brain surgery" at the UCSF Hospital. It was August 2018 and his third brain surgery. A mass had been vigilantly monitored over several years and Kevin's Chemotherapy regimen kept it at bay until it didn't. This time he agreed to surgery and I flew up to be with him. It was a successful surgery and a whirlwind of an experience. His neurosurgeon was confident that the entire tumor was removed. But sadly, two short months later, tumor regrowth was detected.

No!!!!

I took this personally - it was wrong and so unfair! I had just started to settle myself enough to exhale at home and work. The kids started a new school year in August and entered eighth, ninth and twelfth grades. I was adjusting to our set daily schedules and Kevin was just climbing out of recovery mode when he got the devastating news. He committed to stay on at work as long as he could and would leave in the afternoon and head to the oncologists' office. There he'd do his Avastin treatment while tuning in to a DVD movie, or sometimes he'd just sleep. Kevin was now fifty-four.

The chemotherapy was ineffective and a follow-up MRI showed the tumor we didn't want to see. The holidays were on the horizon and I dreaded the approach of Thanksgiving and Christmas, wondering if it was going to be our last one together as a family. I hunkered down while trying to keep up the facade that all was well and smile through it all. Kevin knew he had to do something but subtly stalled the big life and death decisions to allow us time to slow down and be present (just enough) to enjoy the season.

I desperately wanted normalcy, whatever that meant, and tried to project safety and stability for our family and each other. I'd excuse myself and make my way to our bedroom in the early evening where I'd power up the I Pad and search online, yet again for clinical trials, and research topics like "brain cancer miracles" and "innovative cancer therapy." It's been a few months, so what kind of new therapy was out there now? I was deep into my pursuit of miracles, while my family went about their business with homework, scholarship applications, and Instagram. Amidst the busy-ness of life, as usual, there was a sadness factor that began to manifest in me, and the cage of desperation closed in on me again. *We just went through brain surgery! Why are we forced to face this, again, and so soon? God, what is going on?!*

Kevin's Neuro Oncologist at UCSF said that the surgeon who removed the tumor just a few months earlier, confirmed another surgery was possible. This was supposed to be good news. But honestly, rejoicing was equally met with terror. *How can another surgery be the preferred option?* Both Neuro Oncologist and surgeon recommended the procedure immediately and agreed that tumor removal would provide the best possible outcome for Kevin. Kevin was all in. He wanted that out yesterday.

As for me, I was mad and wanted to take down this bully once and for all. I also looked up, incredulously and asked, *"Really, God? Have we not sacrificed enough? Why are you picking on Kevin? Why are you punishing our family? Leave us alone! Phoebe is so close to graduating, do you really need to disrupt our lives again?!"*

Seriously frustrated and despondent, I'd find myself sullen and unable to make sense of what was up or down. I felt heavy-hearted and depressed when I awoke in the morning, and just as sad when

I lay down back to sleep at night. There was no peace to be found, and sound sleep was in short supply. I believed that bad things were to come – pain, suffering, grief, and death.

This was it, I thought.

Once Kevin agreed to another surgery, the wheels were set in motion instantly and brain surgery number four was set for the following week. I crumbled, and my body felt like it went completely limp, like a fully cooked noodle when I received the call that a surgery date had been confirmed. I was at work seated at my desk and immersed in an email response. I heard my personal cell phone ring in my purse and I scrambled to find it tucked beneath the desk. I fumbled to sideswipe and answer in time. It was the UCSF coordinator and she confirmed that Kevin's surgery date was set for the following Wednesday. "Mrs. Furuli, we need to request that your husband be present the day before so that he can get his tests and labs done." I nodded, as though she could see me, then blurted out, "fine, yes, fine."

In six days, my husband would undergo his second brain surgery in six months. Bizarre. Up until that point and I was able to push the threat of life disruption aside and compartmentalize my life – get up, get ready, put my game face on and go to work. Finish work, go home, figure out dinner, and get ready for bed. If life could only be that simple, I wished.

While at work, my responsibilities were weighty and I had a team to lead. I convinced myself that I could mitigate distractions and somehow demonstrate productivity. My priorities were clear; we had work to do, people to meet, stories to tell, donors to inspire and major gifts to secure. *So get going,* I directed myself in my head.

At home, it was even harder and I had major monsters to deal with, psychologically and spiritually, and, what about the imminent logistics? It was a mad scramble as I researched San Francisco lodging – *where would we stay?* Airfares – *did we have enough miles accumulated to cover flights to Honolulu and the mainland?* Insurance – *was the health insurance provider going to authorize another procedure, especially with such short notice?* Medical bills – *what did we still owe from surgery a few months earlier?* On top of that, I had my family to deal with.

Talking with my mom topped my to-do list. I needed my mom so I could sit and talk, cry and unload my darkest fears. She would listen and be my pincushion forced to sustain the sharp piercing to her heart. I needed to ask her to watch my kids and serve as grand-mommy one more time.

Then there was all the devilish junk that surfaced in my psyche, like, *what if Kevin dies and I need to raise the kids by myself now? What if he lives but can't speak, or walk, or remember who we are?* The enemy was working overtime and it felt defeating, it really did. I desperately wanted to rage and unleash my anger on someone or something. I did no such thing. It took everything I had to hold it all together, to put in a full day at work, to make sure the kids felt safe and secure when we were home together and to prepare for what life had in store for us ahead.

Often in the days before we were set to leave for San Francisco, I felt tense, like I was a fragile floating bubble and if someone touched me, I would P-O-P! Thoughts spiraled around me and it was difficult to focus, at work and at home. I carried this heavy weight of needing to be strong, especially for my family, messaging *we've got this; we'll be okay.* If I showed weakness or fear, my kids would pick up on it and feel sad, then Kevin would be affected and feel vulnerable, and this would cause him to be weak. I couldn't afford him to feel weak. I needed him to feel strong and courageous and for our kids to feel brave and hopeful.

Fear and anxiety burdened my spirit and weighed me down big time. I would find myself alone with Kevin, with these feelings of being depressed and bitter. I was mad at him, for taking me on this journey again. This is not the life I wanted, I thought to myself. I felt so helpless and even guiltier for feeling the way I did. I prayed, but it didn't help.

Do You Remember?

One night as we lay in bed, uncomfortably aware of each other's quiet breathing, but wide awake. Kevin leaned over to face me and asked me *"do you remember?"*

My eyes remained closed and I knew exactly what he was referring to. I didn't feel like talking, yet I knew he had things to say and my part was to be present to listen. I was selfish and wanted to neither talk nor listen.

"Yeah, I remember," I said, with my eyes still closed, hoping he'd relent and go to sleep.

Kevin started again and said, *"Andrea, you told me…"*

"I know, I know…. Jesus told me 'to have faith and my prayers will be answered,'" I verbalized before he could finish himself.

Well, my spirit was weak and vulnerable, and my faith was in short supply. I was worn out from bottling up a lot of fear and doubt over the many years. But those words boomeranged back into our lives and gut-punched me where it hurt and got my full attention. I was reminded of how far I've come; how far we've come, together as a family. It's been more than fifteen years since I last walked alone, or thought I walked alone, on my way from Kevin's bedside to my hospital apartment unit. That was in January 2005. I realized back then on my solitary walk that I had divine company; the presence of the Holy Spirit. Since then, we've watched our kids grow up, survived countless arguments, and celebrated numerous birthdays, holidays, and the first high school graduation. All of this beauty was unimaginable in the deep crevices of despair so long ago, and yet here we were. I needed this faith-filled promise, an assurance from God, now more than ever.

"I hear you, Kevin. I hear you," I said, and rolled over and closed my eyes once more.

No Matter What

Family is priority number one.

"No matter what, I want to watch our kids grow up. Whatever it takes and whatever I need to do…that's it, I'm there," Kevin said.

"Okay," I replied.

"I want to see what they do and become. I want to know how close they stay together as grown-ups," he added.

But despite circumstances, he deals with what's before him so that he can look forward to what's ahead, both on earth and in heaven.

I've never met someone as strong-willed as Kevin. As much as he exasperates me at times with his sarcasm, snarky comments, and questionable humor, his devotion and loyalty to family and friends bring me to my knees. There is not a single righteous thing that he would not do for his family or our circle of friends. He takes pride in his family especially and would go to the moon if he could, to ensure the best blessings and outcomes for us.

I think that's the reason why he is here. He desperately wants to stick around to love us and ensure that we are safe and protected. He believes this is his purpose on earth, and I thank our Almighty God for that!

Bracing Again

I found myself facing urgent and unwelcome tasks of talking with docs, reviewing insurance plans, and searching for lodging options, only this time I had less than one week to get it all done. It was overwhelming and I felt smothered beneath the enormity of tasks. One afternoon I came home from work and stood in the living room unable to figure out how to proceed. Kevin was in the shower, the kids were not around, and I cried. I had to find a place to stay in San Francisco and fast.

Six months ago during his last surgery at UCSF, we were blessed with a studio to stay at located about ten minutes away from the hospital. It belonged to extended friends – Mary, Jenn, and Roy. It was in the basement of their three-story home, completely furnished with access to laundry and a beautiful outside patio. It was our temporary sanctuary, a place where Kevin and I felt safe and welcome. I called Mary earlier in the day to ask if we could stay there again. She didn't answer my call and I left a message but didn't hear back from her. I was desperate and on emotion overload.

I stood in our living room feeling sorry for circumstances, and our life together in general. Then *ping*, I received a text from my newly assigned Imerman Angel, Sandy. She messaged to tell me to check my email because she just sent a list of VRBO's near to the hospital. I was confused. She went out of her way to do this without my asking?! She just knew that we'd need a place to stay and looked up places for us. I began to bawl! I remembered thinking, *"who are you and how'd you know I was so stressed about this?"* I pressed send, to text her thanks, and then my phone rang.

Mary was on the other end and asked, "Andrea, is everything okay?" I was so overcome with relief to hear her voice and started to blubber about how the tumor came back and we have to go back to San Francisco for another urgent surgery, blah, blah, blah. I spit out the dates, and she calmly offered for us to stay at their place again. "Andrea, you're welcome to stay as long as needed."

In mere minutes, I went from feeling so completely overwhelmed and defeated to secure, loved and triumphant. Wow! One horrid humbug turned into a beautiful gift, a blessing – we had a place to stay and people around us who cared. My warm salty tears turned into hope-filled water drops. I was in awe. Kevin was still in the shower and had not a clue.

Family Meeting

We convened as a family once more because there was an important matter to be discussed together.

Kevin called the family into the living room again during an evening when we shared with the kids the status of his chemo. It was ineffective and the tumor was growing. He explained to the kids that his biggest desire was to watch them continue to grow up. But for him to do this, he needed to address this tumor threat and that meant another surgery, immediately. We've been through this before and knew all too well the potential dangers and worse case scenarios. He asked the kids how they felt about him going through another surgery and no one said a word.

I asked them instead, "What's your biggest fear if dad has another surgery?"

Ian said, "If dad dies."

Jonah said, "Me too."

Phoebe added, "I'm afraid if something bad happens, that I'll be leaving my brothers all alone to go to college."

We cried.

I told them I was really scared too, and that it was okay to be scared. We are human after all and have emotions. What's important is that together we can be strong and take steps forward.

Kevin added, "This is what we need to do as a family."

Within days, flights were secured, insurance authorizations happened behind the scenes, and Kevin and I tended to official leave requirements on the work front. As a family, we hunkered down and notified our closest circle of peeps one by one.

Departure

Monday morning arrived and our kids got ready for school and left with minimal drama and I was deeply thankful. It was about 7:30 am and we stood at our window and waved as Phoebe reversed the white Explorer onto the street and shuttled her siblings and herself to school.

My mom arrived at our home soon after to take us to the airport. As we stood up to leave, we heard a car drive down our street and stop in front of our driveway…it was Jeannie. I didn't expect to see her and was touched that she came by to spend precious moments with us before we had to leave.

It was a brief visit. Her presence, although unplanned, helped to diffuse my nerves and anxiety. I complained about the wild and abnormal wintry weather conditions in February in the Bay Area. I told her we just saw on the news there were reports of hail and snow along the coast, even. On and on I went about how much I was not looking forward to a likely turbulent flight and how I barely had time to gather cold-weather gear for such cold temperatures. She listened calmly to my rant and then responded, "Hey now, you don't control the weather, so stop worrying. Bring another warm jacket to keep warm, and take your meds before you fly, that's what it's for!" So matter-of-fact. She reminded me that I was human with human feelings, and that was okay. But it's time to move on.

She prayed with us and reminded me **all is well**. This was our special send off and then we were on our way.

We arrived in San Francisco late Monday night during an extreme chilly spell.

Time To Get Up

The piercing ring went off at 4:30 am and was loud enough to wake the entire block up!

I answered the phone, "Phoebe?"

"Mom, are you and dad getting ready?" she asked.

My heart melted and I thought, *Good Lord, it's Phoebe, I love her!* Phoebe called at 2:30 am Hawaii time to speak with us. I was surprised and my throat ached as I barely managed to stifle my tears. I tried to keep the chatter light as she woke up her brothers to say a groggy *"Sup, love you, dad."* No long drawn out discussion, just a short, to the point, "I love you big" message that went both ways.

My daughter was home in the middle of the Pacific Ocean, calling to let her dad know that she loved him, and to let me know that she was with me in spirit! I loved Phoebe fiercely for reaching out as she did, and I knew it meant something very special to her dad, too. Kevin and I were united with taking necessary steps and fully supported one another. But it was still tough being across the ocean, far away from our family and folks who we draw comfort and strength from.

Amidst the anxiety of facing the day, God bridged the expanse of water and reminded me that I was not alone. Receiving the precious message of love delivered through Phoebe was priceless.

I was immersed in my psychological cocoon, as I took in the eerie early morning street scene during or drive to the hospital. We arrived at the hospital via Uber by 5:00 am. Kevin was the first patient checked in, and the following hours were a blur of signing forms and preparing for surgery. Everything happened methodically and Kevin's sister Jennifer and my cousin, Lokemele made their way to share hugs with Kevin before he was wheeled off to the operating room. The nurse warned me that it was my time to leave as well, but I wasn't ready. It was important for Kevin to know that he wasn't alone and that I would be waiting for him when he woke up.

I hate waiting. Some people will never understand how painful and torturous waiting can be. Waiting for the results of an MRI, a call from a doctor, the outcome of surgery, etc. The absolute worst wait is the wait during surgery. I found myself in this intense place of waiting during surgery again; *twice in six months and detested it.*

I kissed my husband and eked out "*I love you...behave in there,*" then the nurses wheeled him off to the operating room. The anesthesiologist put her arm on my shoulder and urged me to take care of myself because Kevin would need me to be strong for him later. I nodded and couldn't make my way out of there fast enough, back to the first floor to the waiting room.

Jennifer and Lokemele were waiting for me. I broke down as Lokemele held me tightly and let me weep and weep and weep. Slowly I looked up at her and managed to say, "Dr. Berger remembered you," and then we laughed so hard.

Flashback: Down She Went

August 8, 2018 [Six months earlier]

Kevin was at UCSF being prepped for his third brain surgery. My little-big (younger-tall) cousin, Lokemele, stood next to me as we squeezed up alongside a wall to allow the prep team ample space to work on Kevin. Everyone was serious and purposeful, and there were lots of needles and tubing being used.

Kevin's neurosurgeon, Dr. Berger arrived to speak with us. This was the first time we met the man who'd be responsible for going in and removing the tumor. He was tall, calm, confident, and we felt at ease with him immediately. He started to pull up the scans of Kevin's current MRI on the computer screen. I've never gotten used to looking at brain pictures and casually looked away. That's when I could feel Loke's head gently lean on my shoulder to comfort me. I leaned back to thank her as the doctor began to explain the next steps. And that's when I pulled back to look up at my tallish cousin, and then stood immobile and stared at her as SHE WENT DOWN!

In a split second, Loke went from standing by my side to lying on the floor. Kevin's whole team went into action and was on the floor right beside her. When she came to several seconds later, she was okay and was able to stand up on her own. She was a little shaken and a bit embarrassed but emphasized to everyone present that she was fine. Our doctor, well, he never missed a beat or showed any hint of nerves whatsoever. He made sure Loke was okay and asked a nurse to escort her downstairs to the waiting room.

During that period of activity, Kevin was stuck lying down in bed and unable to sit up and watch what was happening. He kept looking at me to ask with his eyes, and gesturing "what happened?!" All I could manage was a shrug because I was unsure of what just happened myself. The doc, however, was cool as the coolest cucumber and confidently assured us that he was in control and all was well.

Downstairs, Lokemele couldn't lose the bright sunflower yellow sweater she wore and hide it fast enough. Nor could she escape the teasing from my other cousins Julie, Pat, and Michelle, who kept us company in the waiting room.

Laughter Is Good Medicine

It felt so good to laugh.

I was grateful to have Lokemele and Jennifer with me. The hours passed oh-so-slowly in the waiting room and our shared talks took us up and down, and around again. Their physical presence was soothing and reminded me that I was not alone.

The surgical team communicated hourly with me from the operating room either by a phone call or text. I waited anxiously for each "ping" from the operating room with brief updates, like "Surgery is in process," or "Patient is doing well." A text was overdue and I was incredibly restless because the surgery was expected to be finished already.

I remembered locking my eyes on a woman who walked briskly in my direction. I watched her as she approached and then stood directly in front of me and said *"Andrea?"* I jumped up and thought she was a hospital employee with news to share about Kevin. Instead, she said, *"I'm so glad there was a picture of you so I could see what you look like."* I was confused and crinkled my forehead and looked deeply into her eyes for a clue. Then it dawned on me, and I asked, "Sandy?"

Got Me An Angel

Sandy was my Imerman Angel Mentor. A few weeks earlier I reached out to Imerman Angels, a cancer caregiver support organization and was paired with Sandy. In just a short period, we became friends and communicated frequently over the phone and by text. Sandy was a huge support as I was preparing for the trip and we quickly bonded over our parallel lives and experiences.

Sandy's husband was also a brain tumor patient and had passed away about five years ago. Her story affirmed that I was not the only one out there in the universe who had battled alongside their spouse, felt despair, crawled out from deep dark places seeking hope, and finding it. No, there were others just like me; I was not alone in this journey. Sandy proved this was so. I was deeply grateful for my new friend, more than words can ever express.

In the waiting room, we burst into tears and I eventually got through introductions to Jennifer and Lokemele. Then I felt a tap on my shoulder. Again, I jumped up with the expectation that someone would share news of Kevin's surgery any minute. A young woman with tears in her eyes looked deeply into mine and said that she couldn't help listening in and overheard our story. She explained that her husband was there for a procedure to have cancer removed and the surgery was 100 percent successful. She thanked God and encouraged me to believe in a successful surgery for my husband too. She extended her hand and offered me these golden angel wings, with the word "Love," inscribed on the back.

My eyes remained fixed on hers as I slowly extended my hand to receive what she was offering. I felt a little apprehensive, and the voice in my head said: "I don't know who you are...." Then I quickly broke down and embraced her and cried like a baby. I felt so overcome with emotion and was thankful for the chance to intersect with her at that very moment in time. I remembered looking down again at the angel wings and thought how similar they looked to the Imerman Angel wings...

Then I received the call. The operating room nurse called my cell phone to let me know the surgery was done, Kevin was well, and the doctor wanted to speak with me upstairs. Overwhelmed, I looked to this incredible cluster of ladies assembled in the waiting room and they waved me off. Gratefully, I threw them a kiss and dashed off to catch the elevator back upstairs.

He Is Well

My time with the neurosurgeon was a blur. He said that the surgical outcomes were as good as could be expected and emphasized that brain swelling would take weeks to heal. He also reminded me that Kevin's speech would likely get worse before it gets better.

I'd like to say that I was processing every word the doc was saying but I was not. Once I received the message that Kevin was well, all I could think was *"Hurry up doc, gotta go!"* He finished up, nodded at me, and then suggested that I wait a short while before visiting.

Gasp!

Wait?

Nooooo!!!!

I boldly dashed off to find my husband.

I stepped into Kevin's ICU room and my heart melted when I was met with alert eyes and a *"Hi."*

Kevin told me he was tired and that he was awake for most of the surgery. I stood and stared at him and thought to myself, *"Lord, thank you, thank you, thank you."*

There he lay with his head bandaged, post brain surgery number four, alive, alert and able to speak. **Praise God!** My husband survived! I was so relieved and could hardly contain myself. I put my brave face on, walked over to hold his hand, rested in the moment, then invited his sister and Lokemele up to see him.

I wanted to shout from the rooftops that Kevin made it! I was elated and exhausted. I called the kids. I called my mom. I called my besties, and then I sat and exhaled and cried. In that moment of rest, I sat up and suddenly realized that many people were praying and waiting to hear the news too. Then it hit me – that realization that there were so many, many people out there who lifted Kevin in prayer. Others were on the journey with us. I cannot express the kind of awe and gratitude I felt. I was grateful for each prayer and each person doing the praying.

Bat Cave

Nurses and doctors checked on Kevin constantly in the ICU. They took his vitals, changed his IV, and gave him his medication on a frequent and ongoing basis. It was dark, like a bat cave, yet the machines' incessant beeping kept it noisy, busy and unpleasant. I fought the urge to yank out those uncomfortable-looking tubes, turn off the volume on all-things beeping, and lock the door to prevent the constant barrage of nurses. *Enough already!* I wanted to shout. I got it, he needed to be monitored, but, in my mind, I argued, *let the dude rest*!

The frequent sleep disruptions were rough, but it was even more painful for me to watch when the medical team came by and asked Kevin to answer questions, like, "What is your name? What is your wife's name? Where are you? When is your birthday? Or, what is that?" as they pointed to objects like a pen, the clock on the wall or television. It was awful because he had a difficult time speaking and remembering words. The wait seemed eternal as Kevin struggled to put sounds together, only to be clipped by a nurse or someone who said the word or finished up a sentence for him.

The snappy pants wife was ready to tell the staff where to go. *"Hello, he just had brain surgery, and stayed up, by the way...so cut him some slack,"* is what I wanted to say. Instead, I respectfully nodded, and answered questions and tried to keep my protective bark controlled.

Before surgery, we knew his speech could be impacted more

than it already was. It was still difficult to accept, yet we knew he needed to do what he needed to do, risks included. After surgery, it was evident that his speech was affected and it was heartbreaking to see how frustrated he'd get when nurses and docs would finish his sentences for him, or say words before the sounds could roll off his tongue. My heart was especially sad because while in ICU, he knew who I was, but he couldn't say my name. I smiled, joked about it softly and tried not to cry in front of him.

Meals And Medications

Our time in the hospital revolved around Kevin's meals and medications. In between, we spent hours of channel surfing with the Discovery Channel and drag racing dominating the TV. Now and again, I'd turn off the TV completely and crank up classical music.

I was hypersensitive and tuned in to every little need he expressed. With a nod, I picked up on his request for a sip of water, or the faint movement in his bed caused me to jump up and help him to the bathroom. Our communication transcended volume and we were adept with reading facial expressions, sounds, and gestures.

Time slowed down while we were in the hospital. The hospital stay was four days yet it felt so much more extended. It has been a while since Kevin and I spent uninterrupted time together simply talking and listening to one another without the frenetic busyness that comes with three kids and work. Life has been full, packed to the gills with everything from homework to housework and before fully realizing it, days, months and years have passed.

I'd like to think our family life has always reminded us to be present and grateful, however, I did regret that it took a surgery of the brain, again, to call my husband and me into a setting that forced us to be still, attentive and appreciative of one another.

Added benefits - Thanks to hours of TV viewing, I brushed up on history and sports, my two least favorite subjects.

Naps

I felt safe at the hospital and didn't want to leave. As for Kevin, he didn't want to stay.

Kevin was discharged from the hospital during the early Saturday evening and as much as it was liberating and I looked forward to it, the responsibility terrified me. My role would quickly shift from being an attentive advocate to the sole caregiver, and I was feeling very insecure. The "what if's" were circling like predatory sharks waiting to feast. *What if I get the meds mixed up or give him the wrong dosage? What if he is in pain and I can't make the pain go away? What if his stitches tear and his brain oozes out? What if I can't handle the pressure and take care of him all by myself?*

It's remarkable how quickly the nurses and medical assistants, otherwise strangers, had become like a trusted family. So much so, that I wanted to take a few home with me to help out. I had become attached to many of the nurses and assistants and have such a big space in my heart for all those who dedicate themselves to this profession. My love, respect, and gratitude for the support and care they provide for our loved ones are eternal.

As we got ready to leave, we made our rounds of hugs and *mahalo's* to our new extended family. We were escorted to the lobby where we huddled and waited for our Uber ride to take us back to the apartment sanctuary. I had "to go" meals packed from the hospital cafeteria in preparation for our dinner later and tightly held the bulky bag of meds in my purse. I was now responsible for Kevin's scheduled medications and monitoring dosages, from anti-nausea and anti-seizure steroids to stool softener.

We made it through the next 24 hours, one hour at a time. Funny, it seemed like I was even more tired when we were out of the hospital than when he was a patient. At night it was rough as Kevin woke up hourly to pee. His meds took him to the bathroom numerous times each night, which meant, that lights needed to be turned on and I had to accompany my husband to the loo to make sure he didn't trip or fall.

During the next several days with Kevin, our rhythm continued to be slow and easy; we ate when we were hungry, took short walks around the block when he felt up to it, and enjoyed lots of naps. Okay, I'm the one who maximized on a lot of naps. If he was content with watching pirate ship wreckages on the History Channel, it was my time for a snooze.

Naps were my lifeline when I was able to rest and set my refresh button.

Season of True North

PART TWO

Lost And Found

Where am I?

I am here.

Kevin is there.

The kids are around.

We are all accounted for.

Since we returned home to Hilo, I'm still struggling to figure out what our future looks like. I've returned to work and do my best to pick up where I left off. As for Kevin, he prepares for radiation to be administered locally to prevent another unwelcome tumor recurrence.

We breathe and give thanks.

Charades

The kitchen table seemed so big when the kids were younger and we all had an assigned seat location. Nowadays it seems much smaller and more worn out and without seat assignments. I took a seat, and propped my elbow on the table edge and held my chin as I stared at Kevin across the table from me during an afternoon. We were trying to have a conversation and this could take a while, so I got comfortable.

"Life is like charades with you," I told him. Our conversations often involve a lot of guessing, animated hand gestures and blurting out words and phrases.

Once soon after Kevin was discharged from his first UCSF visit, my dad asked about Kevin's physician and the nationality of his surname. I responded and said, "Is think he's German." Kevin shook his head 'no' and we both looked at him and waited as if he'd soon give us a clue, and he did. Kevin said "war." I repeated softly "war" and asked him, "Do you mean World War One?" and Kevin shook his head again, letting us know we were on the wrong track. My dad said "World War Two" and Kevin nodded his head approvingly. Then I blurted, "Poland" and looked at Kevin for a reaction. He nodded slowly. "I think Dr. Butowski may be Polish," I said.

Kevin's speech has improved, but it's still challenging for him to speak, and for the rest of us to understand him. Our efforts at communicating involve patience and more patience. Communication with Kevin takes hard work, an extra measure of grace, and admittedly, offers some really interesting perspectives. I guess you might say our communication is more *nuanced*.

I warned the kids before we returned home from San Francisco that dad's speech has changed. We hope it will improve as Kevin heals, but it has definitely changed and will take a while if it improves at all. I don't try to cushion the fact that Kevin struggles to find the words and seemingly simple items like "straw" and "watch" were difficult for him and he still struggles to say "UCSF" whenever he is asked about the hospital.

Kevin explained that in his mind, he knows exactly what the words are most times and correlating meanings, but just can't verbalize the word. He will know it immediately once he hears it but may struggle to generate the word first on his own. Sometimes, with a lot of patience the word forms and he can say it. At other times, he cannot, and will let us know. He's developed a lot of tips, tricks, and coping mechanisms along the way. He refers to friends with words that he associates them with, like "aunty," "captain" and "wife" when he can't verbalize names quickly enough.

I'd find myself explaining this to others to soften reactions and provide a safe comfortable space for him to communicate. Again, I'm inclined to protect and shield. *Give him time to answer. He takes a while to recall words and may be silent for a bit. Be patient, and try to fight the urge to say the words or finish a sentence for him.* I can see how it has affected him personally. He is self-conscious and his cocky quips are noticeably less frequent and milder. My son Ian told me, "Do you know that dad wants me to go grocery shopping with him, in case he sees somebody he knows so I can help him talk?" My heart hurt when he shared this with me. Then I thanked God for such a bold son, and for his awareness and his willingness to step in and be a buffer for his dad.

Reading and writing are challenging too. His attempts to text using his phone soon after surgery produced some pretty out there, nonsensical messages, met with a lot of "huh?" from friends and loved ones. I encouraged him to use the Siri feature on his phone to help verbalize his texts, but speaking was hard, too! So it took a while as I responded to messages from folks asking me if Kevin was ok, or telling me they couldn't understand what he wrote. I finally had to explain to Kevin that his writing was loopy and people were confused as much as they were concerned. He became super conversant with Emojis.

Creature Of Habit

Kevin is a true creature of habit. Like clockwork, he rises each morning before the rest of us. He wakes the boys then heads down the hallway to sit at the kitchen table. He gets out his bible, phone and finds his bible reading app. He untangles his earphones then places the small plastic balls in each ear. Now, he's ready to read. Thank goodness for technology.

Kevin can continue to read and keep up with his bible reading/ listening and devotions, with the help of a little voice along the way. He's got the will to read and follows along with the audio. Wow. I find this consistent act of getting up and digging into the word is what grounds him and serves as his directional compass during his day.

When I see my husband faithfully attempt to read and write, I am humbled. I know how hard it is for him, and yet he continues to try. I see a vulnerability equally matched by courage. I pray my kids recognize this and can apply a small measure of humility and resilience when they encounter struggle and hardship because I do not doubt that they will. When that day comes, and their heads are hanging low, I'll be prepared to say, *"Unacceptable. C'mon, look at your dad, he had four surgeries and still gets up to greet the day by reading the bible with his ears. Now tell me again what you're struggling with?"*

I also fall short of excuses when I think of what struggles Kevin faces. In fact, I think I hold myself to higher standards and have become terribly judgmental as a result. I will push myself to do more, to persevere, to get stuff done, even when I don't want to. I'm also extremely critical of people who are weak, flippant and disloyal. I find myself being intolerant of people in my professional and personal spheres who are not committed, kind, positive or passionate. I think to myself how fortunate they are without a life-threatening illness perspective to remind them of our precious existence.

Stripe Head

I was already late when I remembered Kevin's hat on the car seat and I turned back and ran to get it. I reasoned that this was important to grab, just in case he forgot to wear one.

Kevin and Phoebe were already at the Hilo Hawaiian Hotel, to attend the Rotary Club Luncheon, where Phoebe would be recognized for receiving a scholarship. We were so proud and excited for her. She worked hard, and we were delighted to attend the luncheon as happy-proud parents.

I arrived at the dining room and immediately saw them seated way up front, and then I cringed. There was my husband, seated without a hat. I resisted the urge to briskly walk to the table and toss the cap I held in my purse on his head. At that time his hair started to grow back after his surgery and the big scar was hardly visible. Instead, there was a two-inch bald stripe caused by the radiation and wrapped around his entire head.

Local business and community leaders were in the room, many whom I knew personally through work. Before our table host joined us at the table, I softly leaned over and told Kevin that I had his hat in my purse, the one from my car. "Okay. Why, do I need it?" he asked me. I didn't want to be the bossy wife, so I shrugged, and tried to act like it didn't matter to me. But it did at the time. Then he looked at Phoebe, and softly asked, "Phoebe, are you embarrassed by me? Do you want me to put my hat on?" Then my daughter threw me, yes me - the mom, the adult, the working professional, completely under the bus with her words. Phoebe looked up at Kevin and said, "Dad, you're a grown-up. You can make your own decision whether or not to wear your hat."

Yep, just like that.

As much as I was miffed, I was proud of my assertive young adult daughter, who stood up and confidently messaged to her dad, "I love you as is, even with that funky band of baldness around your head."

Can I take some credit for the positive power sass?

Word And Number Play

During dinner, our family would sometimes half-jokingly test Kevin and ask him to recite the days of the week, months, and name each of our birthdays. Most times, he'd start off indignant, chill out, and then sort of play along. Or, he'd be flat out irritated and offended and tell us to leave him alone. On occasion, this banter lead to mischievous play with alphabets, words, and numbers.

"Dad, it's time I get an allowance. O-n-e h-u-n-d-r-e-d-, right dad?" Jonah attempted. Speedily, they'd spell out words, and push the limits to see what Kevin was capable of spelling and making sense of on his own. Ian asked once *"Dad, can we have some C-R-O-W-N -R-O-Y-A-L?"* as he refilled our glasses with wine. I looked up at him and gave him the stink eye. He's our sly one.

We'd also play Yahtzee and I'd be the designated scorekeeper. Incredulously, my husband leaned over numerous times to check the scorecard and see what category he still needed to fulfill. In doing so, he'd nonchalantly catch my addition errors. The first time he pointed out a mistake, I disregarded him as the spouse with brain surgery and graciously thanked and ignored him. He persisted to challenge me to look at the score and sure enough, I inflated my score by two whole points! I whimpered my way to the corner and have paid careful attention since.

I've witnessed how amazing the brain is over the past year, especially. I watched over my husband's shoulder as he read aloud from the bible once, and was struck when he verbalized the word "inheritance" when the actual word read "riches." He comes up with similar words and phrases frequently and doesn't realize that what he's verbalizing is not exactly what is written, although it means the same thing. Another time, I tried to gain Kevin as an ally so we could together convince Jonah to move into his sister's room after she headed to college. Kevin took Jonah's side instead and told me, "I don't blame him for wanting to stay on the deck. It's cooler out there and he's 'hot like butter.'" I asked, "Did you mean hot-blooded?" And he said, "Yeah, that's what I said." But he didn't say what he thought he said.

Mixed up phrasing happens all the time. Recently as he recounted a story, he paused and told me, "So…big whole story short…" Our eyes met, I smiled, leaned in and chuckled. Then I nodded, and said, "Yeah….Go on."

Cheers And Tears

Kevin and I reached our first high school graduation milestone as parents, finally! I watched with tears in my eyes as Phoebe's name was announced and she made her way up to the platform in her crisp white gown and brand new heels to receive her diploma. All of the ire and irritability from earlier in the day just melted away while I watched her smile and wave at us as she walked by. But honestly, it took a lot to get to that joy-filled mom point.

Earlier in the day, we all got dressed up and loaded the van with our bags filled with lei to share at our family's first high school graduation ceremony. Kevin, Ian, Jonah and I dropped Phoebe off at the designated site, and then dutifully stood in line for hours to ensure we had premium seats. The wait seemed eternal, not to mention it was miserably muggy with no afternoon shade to be found. I was hobbling around with a bright purple foot cast and sought out the handicap entrance in hopes I'd be allowed early entry. No such luck.

All of the entrances finally received approval to open the gates and people poured in from all sides. I watched the frenetic dash to the inner stadium, while our gate remained closed; they had the wrong key and could not unlock the gate. Others in line with me stood in disbelief as the security guard was summoned to assist our station attendant. My nerves were frazzled and I could barely keep quiet. *We've been waiting in this hot afternoon sun for more than an hour; my foot aches and my armpits are drenched! Now let me in so I can get seats to see my daughter walk the line!* At last, someone arrived with a master key and I made a beeline to find the perfect seats for our group.

Ian accompanied me, and we boosted to the floor area to reserve a total of ten seats for our family and friends joining us. I exhaled after we secured our space and eagerly awaited the arrival of each person. We had a power squad, including my mom and my sister-friends, present to cheer and tear with me!

Following the program and awarding of diplomas, there was mass chaos. Graduates and their families scurried about to find each other and thankfully, we were located nearby so Phoebe was an easy target. She was presented with leis stacked up to her chin and then buzzed off to find more of her friends. The adrenaline was intense with horns sounding, congratulatory shouts, and lots of hugs and well wishes exchanged between graduates, parents, and friends. It was exhilarating, yet I was thankful when we were able to exit this scene and call it a night. Most importantly, graduation activities were underway and would provide graduates with a safe place to go and expend their energy allowing me some restful shuteye.

God bless graduates.

Good night.

Success

I don't ever want to go through another brain cancer diagnosis or experience another surgery with my family. Never. Ever. Again.

Immediately after I returned from the last trip to San Francisco, I was on a personal crusade to save Kevin and my family from future threats and to do so, we needed to find a new house. I rationalized that a new home would provide a fresh start, and clean healthy living space, and a new fresh life. I desired more than anything else to remove our family from this old tainted past and believed a new house would make us happy and healthy. This goal consumed me and I took my entire family on a desperate house-hunting rollercoaster ride.

Once I finished the loan prequalification process, we sought out a realtor and lined up homes to look at. Throughout a couple of months, we ended up visiting dozens of homes. I fell for a property with an ideal yard and garden space attached to a very dated house that required extensive renovation work. I was hooked on the potential offered by the larger lot size that was completely fenced, which would be premium yard territory for the dogs. I could also imagine myself tending the gardens and willing to overlook all of the work needed to be done to make the place livable for the family. That's how desperate I was to move.

Kevin did not stand in my way and obliged the entire time. He knew my feelings and genuinely wanted to make me happy. So he and the boys accompanied me to many homes and walked through many yards, then waited expectantly for the sale to close once our offer was accepted. Then all of a sudden, I got cold feet and pulled out at the very last minute.

I couldn't go through with it. I knew all the while that I was selfishly imposing this "new home, new me" dream on my entire family, but couldn't stop myself. I believed it would be a good thing for everyone, but I was doing it from a place of desperation. I finally had to stop, acknowledge my sense of urgency, stare it down, take a breath and think clearly. And I had to apologize to my family for taking them on such a crazy random rocky ride. I tried my best to explain that I didn't want to return to the same place, in my mind, in my heart, and even living space.

That's when I was forced to slow down just enough to pause. I was reacting to my deep realization that our time together was precious and quieted my thoughts and asked Kevin, "What are our priorities? What are your goals?" He said, "Phoebe going to college, that's a success." I shook my head and said that's not what I asked. I was trying to get him to think about our priorities and what's important for us to commit to. He said, "You asked me what my goals are. Seeing the kids graduate high school and go off to start college, that's a success. *To help them succeed is my goal.*"

"Got it," I said and nodded. In my heart I thought, that's so profound.

Season Ahead

Go On

Kevin's selflessness has been a constant during our journey and intangible anchor for our family, honestly. That's the source of strength that I've drawn from during the years to equip myself and family for whatever circumstances we faced.

It's a new season for us. Together, we escorted Phoebe to college in Oregon as she stepped onto George Fox University as a freshman. I'm forced to face how life rolls forward and find myself adjusting to having two teenage fellas left at home. As a family, we continue to figure out ways to get along and how best to support Kevin and each other.

More and more in my quiet moments, I have come to realize how far I've traveled, on my own, with my husband and together with my family. I'm also reminded of how much mercy and grace have been present during my story/our story all along. Events in the past, present, and future, have been masterfully stitched together to become my life storybook using the thread of goodness and grace to bind it.

I can visualize how a divine hand has been holding our family together and makes me want to fall to my knees with a heart bursting with love and gratitude. There were countless times when my fear and doubt prevented me from trusting and leaning into faith, and that struggle continues today. It is a constant challenge to surrender self, acknowledge my human fragility and call on the sovereignty of my savior to work all things for good.

I don't know what tomorrow holds and learned early on that life is uncertain. But, despite the uncertainty, we each have a choice on how to live with this uncertainty. I've chosen to live fully. It's not easy. Living fully demands love and faith, even when we don't feel up to be loving and faith-filled. In those times of weakness, we must prepare our hearts and minds for a battle like no other, where we will pour everything we have to conquer the enemy. For me, I've relied on love, faith, hope, and courage to help me in times of trials; to battle and **triumph** from glory to glory.

Acknowledgments

This book project was Holy Spirit-lead and aided by special people who provided the support to begin the work, and the grit to finish it.

I am indebted to my family, who stood in agreement and allowed pieces of our story to be shared through my lens as wife and mom. Together, we hope that something contained in these pages might serve as a source of hope, comfort, and encouragement for others.

An extra measure of gratitude to my cheerleaders; I am grateful for the boosts that stirred my heart and compelled me to get started and keep going. Aloha-flowing hugs to the incredible group of lady warriors with whom I share the banner of caregiver – you have given me a source of strength and hope during times with I needed it desperately. As I wrote, your faces and stories coaxed me to keep writing. Pastor Lynn, your words were especially meaningful and made me believe that my story is worth sharing.

To our extended family of medical professionals – my heart overflows with thanksgiving. Kevin's team of doctors, nurses, specialists, technicians and advocates is expansive and we are indelibly touched by your care and kindness through the years. Our world is a better place because of your hearts, skills and compassion.

Printed in the United States
By Bookmasters